BLOOD IN THE TRENCHES

A MEMOIR OF
THE BATTLE OF THE SOMME

CAPTAIN A. RADCLYFFE DUGMORE

Pen & Sword
MILITARY

This edition published in 2014 by

Pen & Sword Military
An imprint of
Pen & Sword Books Ltd
47 Church Street
Barnsley
South Yorkshire
S70 2AS

This book was first published as 'When the Somme Ran Red'
by George H. Doran Company, New York, 1918.

Copyright © Coda Books Ltd.
Published under licence by Pen & Sword Books Ltd.

ISBN: 9781783463114

A CIP catalogue record for this book is available from the British Library

All rights reserved. No part of this book may be reproduced or transmitted in any form or by any means, electronic or mechanical including photocopying, recording or by any information storage and retrieval system, without permission from the Publisher in writing.

Printed and bound in England
By CPI Group (UK) Ltd, Croydon, CR0 4YY

Pen & Sword Books Ltd incorporates the imprints of Pen & Sword Aviation, Pen & Sword Family History, Pen & Sword Maritime, Pen & Sword Military, Pen & Sword Discovery, Pen & Sword Politics, Pen & Sword Atlas, Pen & Sword Archaeology, Wharncliffe Local History, Wharncliffe True Crime, Wharncliffe Transport, Pen & Sword Select, Pen & Sword Military Classics, Leo Cooper, The Praetorian Press, Claymore Press, Remember When, Seaforth Publishing and Frontline Publishing

For a complete list of Pen & Sword titles please contact

PEN & SWORD BOOKS LIMITED
47 Church Street, Barnsley, South Yorkshire, S70 2AS, England
E-mail: enquiries@pen-and-sword.co.uk
Website: www.pen-and-sword.co.uk

Being a very egotistical account of my own personal experiences and observations from the early days of the war in Belgium to the Great Battle of the Somme in July, 1916

A Radclyffe Dugmore
  Capt.

As a token of admiration this book is dedicated with all humility to the glorious memory of the officers and men of the King's own Yorkshire light infantry who fell in the Battle of the Somme, and to the others who made the supreme sacrifice in the cause of humanity.

Contents

Foreword 6

Part One

Chapter I	In Belgium - A Prisoner 10
Chapter II	Wounded at Alost 23
Chapter III	In England - from Civilian to Soldier 32

Part Two

Chapter IV	Rejoining My Battalion 39
Chapter V	First View of the Trenches 45
Chapter VI	At Bécordel - Strafed 51
Chapter VII	In the Front Line Trenches 62
Chapter VIII	Preparing for the Great Offensive 77
Chapter IX	Hell Let Loose 95
Chapter X	Battle of the Somme - The Great Day 103
Chapter XI	A Bad Night Among the Shells 114
Chapter XII	Captured Lines and Prisoners 120
Chapter XIII	The Toll of Battle 129
Chapter XIV	Rest - and Return to the "Show" 138
Chapter XV	A Hot Corner - Gassed 146
Chapter XVI	The Pivot 156

Foreword

The Second Battle of the Somme In Relation to the British Offensive of 1916

WHEN THE GERMANS undertook their great offensive against France in 1914 their plan was, of course, to overrun with the utmost speed, a sufficiently large area of the country to ensure an almost immediate and complete victory. Paris was the first important objective. The attainment of this was to have been followed rapidly by a drive against the sea-port towns on the English Channel, with the obvious effect of preventing Great Britain from coming to the assistance of her ally. In planning this ambitious scheme of conquest the German strategists realized the possibility of failure and selected as their strategic line of defense, in case they were forced back from Paris, the region east of the Somme and northward from Curlu, taking in the line which included the villages of Mametz, Fricourt, La Boisselle, Ovillers, Thièpval, Beaumont, Hamel, Gommecourt, and on in a more or less northerly direction to the coast.

This line was chosen with the greatest possible skill. It followed the series of ridges and hills and thus gave command of the country to the west; in other words, any attack against the Germans would have to be made uphill, always a difficult undertaking. Besides the natural strength of the position the line was made still more secure by the employment of every device known to military science, so that it was regarded as an almost impregnable system of trenches. This then was the line we were to attack in July, 1916, largely with the idea of relieving the pressure that was being exerted against Verdun.

In the following pages I have attempted to give some idea of how at least on one part of the front, the offensive was carried out. It was written before the recent gigantic German attacks, which, unfortunately, have succeeded in forcing us back to a line which in part is west of the position we occupied in June, 1916. Whether or not we could have avoided yielding this ground I am not in a position to know, but there is every reason to believe that to have held our line would have involved the sacrifice of such an immense number of lives that it was considered wiser to give up the ground, at the same time making the Germans pay a toll in lives out of all proportion to the value of the territory they have gained.

Whether or not this is Germany's final effort none of us can tell. The common idea is that if it fails the German people will demand peace, as they will be sickened by the ghastly slaughter, which has surpassed anything the world has ever known. This theory is not generally believed by those who are in the best position to judge, so it is not wise for us to make plans based on the supposition that peace is near. Such action would mean the delaying of the most necessary war preparations, and this is exactly what the Germans are most anxious to have happen. It is the work of their propagandists to make people believe that the war will very soon be finished, so that we shall slow down on the manufacturing of war material and the training of men. It is well, therefore, to guard against all stories dealing with early peace, and if possible try to trace the origin of such stories. The source will in nearly all cases be found to be German, or what is equally vile, pacifist, for the pacifist is quite as dangerous as the pro-German in our midst. He would have us, among other things, conclude a shameful peace on *any* terms, he would have us barter our heritage of liberty and freedom for whatever disgraceful form of government the unprincipled military power of Germany would impose on us, so that those who have died for our cause would have died in vain.

Unfortunately so little information has been given to the public regarding the exact position occupied by the Allies at the present time that it is extremely difficult to form any accurate opinion of the situation. Apparently the Germans are in possession of the country east of a line running south from Bailleul to Mourlancourt, from which point it appears to swing slightly westerly, curving round to Montdidier. Albert is in the hands of the enemy, and the famous statue of the leaning

Virgin, mentioned in another chapter, has probably already been melted down for the purpose of making munitions. From Albert to Corbie runs the little river Ancre, which is bordered by more or less swampy ground from Ville to where it joins the Somme. On either side of the valley is high rolling ground, most of which is under cultivation, with patches of woodland here and there. It is ideal country for open warfare. Judging from the accounts that have been published, I am inclined to believe that we still hold the north side of the valley as far as Heilly, or perhaps a little farther toward Corbie, but whether we are in possession of the high ground which overlooks the town from the east and south I do not know. Everything depends on this, as these hills completely dominate the town. Should Corbie fall, the position of Amiens will be very serious and for many reasons the Germans are most anxious to force us out of this important town and railway centre.

From Corbie to Amiens there is a wide belt of low and somewhat swampy land following the river. This is controlled to some extent by a range of hills on the north side and to a less extent by lower rolling ground on the south, so that unless the Huns cross the Somme, and attempt to outflank us, the attack on Amiens would be difficult and very costly. It is quite impossible to make predictions with any degree of accuracy, but though the situation at the present moment is serious, the optimistic tone of the French and British commanders as expressed in the newspapers should give us reason to believe that the great German offensive is doomed to ultimate failure, even though it gains a considerable amount of territory.

From a sentimental point of view we feel very deeply having to yield ground that was won at such a terrible cost in lives and energy; to those of us who took part in the 1916 advance it is a very great blow, for we believed that if once the Bapaume region was taken we would be able to hold it against any forces the Germans could bring against us. Through the greater part of the regained area the work of reconstruction had been carried on with the utmost energy. The shell-torn ground was being levelled and made ready for cultivation, roads were repaired and railways laid. And now, not only has all this work been either destroyed or taken over by the Germans, but many villages, which hitherto had been peacefully occupied by the French people, who had always treated us with such kindness, have been wrested from us, and the chances are very great that the wretched people will never again see anything but the ruined remains of their former homes.

Apart from the actual material loss there is the terrible thought that the graves of our poor Dead are desecrated by the very presence of the Hun. At least we had hoped that the bodies of those who made the Great Sacrifice for the cause of Right might have been allowed to rest undisturbed in their simple graves. But such apparently was not to be, and we can only pray that the time is not far distant when the Hun and all he stands for shall be driven forever from the soil of France and Belgium. Before that day comes we must expect to go through periods of great strain and anxiety. Our endurance will perhaps be tested almost to the point of breaking, but the knowledge of the righteousness of our cause, of the greatness of our resources, and above all, the wonderful spirit and determination of our men, who are engaged in the fighting, and the no less wonderful spirit of those who, though forced to remain at home, are so generously backing up the fighting forces, make ultimate victory a matter of certainty. The Hun can never triumph. Even though he were to force us out of France; even though he were to capture Paris, that will not bring him nearer to victory. So long as a drop of living blood remains in France and Great Britain the war must continue. America's gigantic preparations are bearing fruit, her limitless resources will, as time goes on, make her power more and more a factor in the task of defeating the Hun. She has championed the cause of World freedom, and she will not rest until that cause has been won, and adequate measures taken to ensure a lasting peace, a peace which will guarantee safety for even the smallest and most helpless of nations. We owe nothing less than this to our heroic Dead, and we should never dare look on the little White Crosses that mark their last resting places if we failed in this sacred obligation.

A. R. D.

PART I

Chapter I
In Belgium - A Prisoner

BEFORE DEALING WITH my somewhat limited experiences and impressions of the Great War I feel that a word of explanation as to how at my age I happened to give up my peaceful occupation as a private citizen and join the army will not be altogether out of place, especially as it relates to that ghastly period of the war, the devastation of Belgium.

It will be remembered that within a few days after Great Britain's declaration of war against Germany accounts of the atrocities committed by the invaders of Belgium were circulated throughout the country. We were incredulous at first, no one believed that a great nation could be guilty of the horrors attributed to Germany, and yet evidence was not lacking to show that the worst stories were to a great extent true. Throughout my life, which has been devoted to the study, of outdoor natural history, I have always found it advisable to see before believing, in other words to verify reports before regarding them as facts. Thus it happened that on August 14th, 1914, I made my way to Belgium armed with a camera and a large and most imposing British passport.

Ostend was my first objective, and I found the famous watering place in a very peaceful condition, but there was a great deal of suppressed excitement, and the conversation was only of the war and what the Germans were doing in other and less fortunate parts of the country. The town was more or less bedecked with the flags of the Allies, and various proclamations regarding the duties of the people and other matters, together with coloured posters of the uniforms of friendly and enemy soldiers were conspicuous in every street. Later on refugees from various parts of the invaded country drifted into Ostend, and arrangements were hastily made to feed and house the unfortunate homeless people. Private individuals as well as the Bed Cross undertook this work of relief, but it put a great strain on the resources of the town. There was a rumour that Brussels was to be taken, so I went there and found the amusing, even pitiful, spectacle of ridiculous little barricades thrown across various main streets. These were guarded by members of the *Garde Civique*. The whole thing struck me as being absurd, to think that such childish efforts could stay the troops of the most highly organised military organisation the world had ever known. Reason fortunately prevailed and these futile preparations were abandoned. Sixteen hours after I left the city the Germans entered, so I missed the great but lamentable sight.

I returned to Ostend in time for a small taste of excitement when a few Uhlans made what was apparently a reconnaissance of the town. They were warmly received by the Belgians who met and engaged them on the outskirts. The town was in a badly frightened condition. Allied flags were hastily concealed. All who could were flocking to the steamer landing in hopes of getting away to England. Frantic efforts were made to get hold of money, English gold realising as much as 35 francs for the sovereign. I was eating my breakfast at the Hotel Maritime when the excitement outside In the square suggested a new development of affairs. A few minutes later some Belgian soldiers passed through the dining-room, leading a highly indignant German officer on whose arm was the sign of the Bed Cross. It appeared that he had been caught red-handed in the act of trying to shoot some Belgians. One of his captors was carrying the revolver. Soon a couple of badly wounded Uhlans were brought in and put on board the steamer for England. It is a pleasure to record that they were treated with the utmost care. This apparently was all we were to see of the skirmish. If I remember correctly about nine Germans were killed and three or four Belgians. It brought home to the people of Ostend that the war was very near. But their faith in France and Britain was great, help would come in time they felt sure. Alas they were doomed to disappointment.

From Ostend I moved to Ghent, and while there paid several visits to Termonde during the various periods of its destruction, and what a pitiful sight it was. The wretched little town of some 1600 houses was almost a complete wreck. Over 1200 houses were destroyed, whole streets were simply piles of bricks and broken stones, mingled here and there with remains of bodies and torn clothing. A few houses stood intact for on their doors was the magic chalk mark that good people lived there - in other words Germans, or at least German sympathisers, or still worse, spies. The churches and convents were ruthlessly destroyed and this was not because the churches being usually high were places of observation, for in one case the little low built chapel in the square surrounded by the houses of the old women who were supported by the town was burned, though it could offer no possible point for observation, while at the entrance to the square was the chalked order, that, as only very old women lived there the houses need not be destroyed. The Germans seem to have had the idea that by destroying the churches they were taking the heart and soul from the people. It is one of their many great psychological mistakes.

The last time I visited Termonde was a Sunday two or three days after the most recent destructive visit made by the Germans. I had with great difficulty obtained a pass. In fact it was granted only by explaining how necessary it was that people in England and America should know exactly what was happening to Belgium, so that they could help in whatever ways were possible, and that I would send or take these photographs directly to England. It made one's heart sick to see the misery of the wretched Termonde people. They seemed to be stunned. Of course during the bombardment, and subsequent incendiary work, practically all of the inhabitants had fled. On this Sunday the country seemed so quiet and peaceful that they returned as though in hopes that it had all been a dream, and they wandered about among the blackened ruins trying vainly to discover what had but a few hours before been their homes. What had they done that they should be so treated? They were peaceful people working only that they might live in their simple homes. Why then should these German devils come without cause or provocation and ruin them? One nice looking woman, who was carrying a tiny baby in her arms, pointed to a pile of bricks and said, "My little baby was born there three weeks ago and now I have not even a cradle for her. My God, this is not war, this is the work of the devils," and she was right.

As I wandered through the scene of desolation I came upon a building, two-thirds of which had fallen, and its walls were pitted with shot. All that remained was a small wine and coffee shop. A voice called as I passed, "Come in, you are a friend - you are English. Have a cup of coffee. It is all I have left to offer, but you are welcome to it."

I accepted the welcome refreshment from the old couple who were happy to find even a part of their house more or less intact. When I offered to pay for the coffee they refused to accept any money saying that soon the English were coming over to help them and they would then be happy. Poor people, I wonder what has become of them and if they are still waiting for the help they were expecting over three years ago.

After crossing the river where my car was waiting I engaged in conversation with a Belgian officer who told me how the soldiers had done all in their power to protect the town. The odds against them were overwhelming. He pointed with pride to the decapitated tower of the *Place de Ville*, It appears that the Germans had managed to place a machine gun in the belfry and it must have been a difficult task. I had been up there only a couple of days earlier and had great difficulty in getting my camera up to the top. The officer who was in the field artillery told his men that he wanted the gun destroyed. Two shots striking simultaneously cut off the upper half of the tower completely and with it the machine gun and crew. This same officer told how two German officers wishing to examine carefully the river banks, came out in the open street, carrying in their arms a baby, evidently hoping by this means to protect themselves. A man who was an expert shot was detailed to attend to the case with the result that the officer carrying the baby was shot through the head. The baby escaped unhurt while the second officer hurriedly sought the nearest shelter.

It was some days after this visit to Termonde that in company with my friend Arthur H. Gleason (whose splendid unselfish work in Belgium and France is well known) I visited a convent in which I had been told there was a young girl who had been terribly maltreated by German soldiers. She was lying then at the point of death, a victim of some twenty human devils, who forced the father and mother to be present that they might witness their daughter's ruin. This is not a nice subject to write about, and I merely touch on it to show one of the causes of my joining the army.

Near Ghent is, or rather was, the little village of Melle. It happened to be in the way of the German army of invasion. Early one morning reports came into Ghent that severe fighting was in progress. My car not being available I hired a carriage to which was more or less attached a dilapidated horse, and which took us along the road toward Melle. We passed numbers of Belgian soldiers, ill equipped but always cheerful, going forward. Also numbers of wounded men being brought back. They were in all sorts of vehicles, from fine motor cars to springless waggons, and it was indeed a pitiful sight. Two cases I can even now remember clearly were men, one with his lower jaw completely shot away, and the other terribly wounded in the body, lying on the top of an old fashioned covered carriage. The inside was full to its utmost capacity with wounded. Every jolt over the rough paved roads sent a shock of pain through their torn bodies. They endured it heroically, for it was better than falling into the hands of the Germans whose treatment of Belgian wounded was in so many cases absolutely brutal. But what a contrast were these makeshift vehicles to the ambulances of the present time, pneumatic tired and smooth running, and equipped with stretchers, on which the wounded are borne with the minimum of pain. Conditions have greatly changed since those days of trial.

By the time we had gone within two or three miles of Melle the sounds of battle filled the air. Not battle as we now know it with its overwhelming voice of heavy artillery, but chiefly the rifle, and the machine gun with its regular rapping death-dealing shots. Now and then light artillery punctuated the sound, and we wondered whether this meant that the Germans were advancing on Ghent. No one seemed to know much of what was going on. The peasants stood about in silent groups, worried at the prospect of what fate had in store for them. Some few went on with their regular work apparently deaf to the unceasing clatter of shot. It did not seem advisable for us to proceed any further along the road by carriage, so, much to the driver's relief, for he thought we were urging him straight into the jaws of death, we told him to hide his vehicle in a narrow alley, and leaving the motion picture camera in his care we walked forward armed only with a small pocket camera.

Before long the glint of a lance caught our eyes, and we saw what we thought was a German Uhlan peering from among the trees at the entrance of a big estate. He was about 800 yards distant. How strange it was to see this silent evidence of the war, this human being stalking his own kind. It gave me a curious thrill of excitement for it was practically the first time I had been hunted by a soldier, a man trained to hunt his fellow man. And I was among those he was watching. He was dressed in the elusive grey-green uniform of the German army, and the colours blended among the trees so that he was scarcely visible. Silently he had come and as silently he vanished from our view.

After he had disappeared we looked further along the road and saw clearly a group of cavalry, all carrying their long tubular lances. Being filled with curiosity we wanted a nearer view, and decided to walk slowly in their direction. Before we had advanced more than three or four hundred yards we were startled by the clatter of horses' hoofs behind us, and turning we were very much upset by seeing three mounted men in field green uniforms following us. It was too late to attempt concealment and we dared not turn back. The only possible course was to continue forward as though we were not afraid, though I do not mind confessing I was so thoroughly frightened that my knees trembled violently. Before we had gone far the three hussars, as they turned out to be, overtook us and wanted to know who we were and what we were doing. I acknowledged myself an Englishman while my friend said he was American, whereupon one of the three spoke to us in good English, and told us he had been in New York for some years.

All this time we were approaching the cross roads while we talked in quite a friendly way about New York. As we drew near to the group of about a dozen, which proved to be of the same regiment as our escorts, our three formed up, one on either side, and one behind, and I had horrible thoughts of what might be in store for us. We were taken before the officer who on hearing our nationalities addressed us in perfect English. He was most polite and told us that for a number of years he had lived in England, had been to Oxford, and finished by saying that he hoped the war would soon end as he was very much attached to English life and was most anxious to get back to his friends there. He declared that he thoroughly disliked the idea of fighting us but that he had been recalled, and could not do other than obey. Altogether he seemed a thoroughly decent sort of Saxon. We asked whether we could go forward as we both were very anxious to see a fight.

"You can't go yet," he replied, "as you would most certainly be shot, but later, when things have quieted down, you may perhaps be able to go with safety, and by the way do you happen to have any cigarettes, I have not had a decent smoke for a week?"

So I handed him a nearly full box, telling him to keep them, for I fully expected to be back in Ghent within a few hours. I then asked if he had any objection to my taking a photograph of him and his men. He did not object at all, in fact he was very much pleased.

"Don't forget to send me prints after the war," he said, as he wrote his name and address on the envelope containing my passport.

"I shall be delighted to do so only, of course, there won't be any Germans left when we have finished with you."

He replied, "You mean there won't be any English left."

How little either of us realised what was before us, and how soon that war would develop into such gigantic proportions. That it would last even until Christmas of that year did not seem probable, for we in general knew nothing on the subject. We all thought that with modern methods conditions would be made so intolerable that no country could endure the slaughter which apparently must result. Only those who were in high command, and who had studied the subject, understood that there was a probability of the war continuing for many years. Did not people regard Lord Kitchener as a pessimist when he said we must prepare for at least three years? That period has passed and the end is not yet in sight. But to go back to our interview with the Saxon officer.

By half past three the sounds of fighting had subsided. Only an occasional shot disturbed the stillness of the afternoon. We were told that it would be reasonably safe to go forward and foolishly enough we went. Our way led us through a small one-street village which had not been molested. The people stood about in groups talking over what had been going on in the nearby village of Melle, and we gathered from what they said that the place had been completely destroyed, and a great many civilians and troops killed. While pressing along the road between the two villages a German sentry warned us not to walk on the paved part as he said it was mined. Why he let us pass I cannot understand, but he asked no questions. Evidently he imagined that we had a right to be there.

Soon we came on signs of the recent conflict, buildings burned or destroyed by shell, bodies of Belgian troops and occasional peasants in civilian garb, lying about in the queer distorted attitudes so common on the battlefield. Here and there the carcass of a cow or a pig lay across the road, often with the body of a soldier lying against it showing that the man had been foolish enough to trust to the soft body for protection against the enemy's bullet.

All that remained of the village of Melle was the row of slowly burning cottages. A truly desolate sight. I was in the act of securing a photograph of the scene, in the foreground of which lay a poor Belgian soldier slowly burning, when a German cyclist approached without my seeing him. Quickly dismounting he seized my camera, and was about to break it, when I made him understand that it contained the photograph of one of his officers. At first he seemed incredulous, but on being shown the name and address written in the officer's own handwriting he somewhat reluctantly handed back the camera. But strange to say, he did not seem in the least surprised and never even asked us what we were doing.

Had we possessed a particle of intelligence we would have been satisfied with what we had seen and returned, instead of which we very foolishly continued on the road to trouble with the result that within a few minutes we were taken prisoners by a number of soldiers, who, asking no questions, led us straight to their officers.

The prospect looked very dark and I must confess to having experienced a most disagreeable sinking sensation in the region of my heart. That we should come out of it alive did not seem possible. I, at any rate, was an Englishman, and had been seen trying to use a camera in a region that could not by any stretch of imagination be considered healthy for photographic work. The interrogations to which we were subjected by the group of ferocious unsmiling officers were brief. Gleason said he was an American out on newspaper work, while I proclaimed my British nationality, showed my imposing passport, and said that a thirst for knowledge and a roving disposition had brought me to Belgium to look on. The Germans have no sense of humour. They never so much as smiled, but brusquely ordered us both into a field and placed us under guard. Apparently we were not to be shot - just yet. Pretty soon a couple of large motors came along filled with a grand array of German staff officers. They stopped near us and began discussing the name of the village which their troops had so thoroughly destroyed. Evidently there were several different opinions, and, strange to say, I was called up and asked the name. I told them quite truthfully that I was a stranger, and so I was dismissed, and not even thanked for giving such valuable information.

Life was getting to be very monotonous and we could elicit no information from our silent guards. Once an officer came by and we asked him if we could go as we were tired of doing nothing. His only reply was a growl which seemed to mean, "No, damn you," so we stayed. With the approach of evening other prisoners were added to the haul until we numbered nearly thirty. The newcomers being all Belgians who like ourselves imagined they were doomed to decorate the front of a convenient wall. Under the circumstances they were fairly cheerful, though there was no undue hilarity noticeable.

Shortly before sunset we were greatly interested in watching the German troops arrive, some 15,000 in all. Everything was done in the most orderly manner. Their neat bivouac tents were arranged in straight lines. Their camp-cookers came up, and rations were distributed in a most business-like way. Few commands were given and those in a surly, bullying tone. Some of the officers carried small whips with them, evidently with the idea of accentuating orders. What a marked contrast to the way our officers treat their men!

The troops were extremely well clothed and equipped but were by no means a cheerful lot. There was none of that jolly banter that is always to be found among our fellows. Not even any of that inevitable good-natured grumbling in which our men always indulge, especially when there happens to be no reason for it. I have always noticed that the British Tommy's grumbling, or grousing, as he prefers to call it, is in inverse ratio to cause. In other words the more comfortable he is the more he complains, while when everything is miserable, when it pours with rain, when the twelve-mile march measures twenty, even when his rations fail to turn up at the proper hour, he searches thoroughly for whatever there may be of a funny side to the situation, and promptly blossoms forth into song and jest - all of which is a Godsend, and helps so greatly to make the burdens as light as possible. The German soldiers struck us as perfectly trained but rather dull, and altogether too quiet. The food served to them from the camp cookers was, as far as we could see, a thick stew which smelt rather good. There was also a hot beverage, which I suppose was coffee, but our hosts were thoroughly inhospitable, and never offered us any sort of refreshment, though I would have given a good deal for a drink of cold water.

Shortly before dark we were moved forward, and placed immediately behind a long straight freshly made trench. This was scarcely three feet deep, and the parapet about two feet high, composed of earth and coils of wire, taken from a nearby concrete factory. In the trench the men placed a lot of straw taken from a poor peasant's wheat stack, and there they slept with their rifles all laid on the parapet.

How strangely unlike the trench methods of to-day! Around us a strong guard was placed, with one sentry in the centre of our little group. To make sure that we would not escape a lantern was hung so that we could be easily watched. The extraordinary precautions for our safety struck us as comical and I even ventured to laugh whereupon I received strict injunctions that laughing was forbidden. We were forced to lay flat, and the space allowed was so small that we were actually on top of each other, and were miserably uncomfortable and very cold. One human sort of sentry slipped a sheaf of oats to me and it made life more endurable, besides furnishing pie with food, for I peeled the husks and ate the grain. My light breakfast of the early morning was so very remote that my stomach had completely forgotten it.

One thing which rather disturbed our equanimity was the fact that, so far as we could understand, we were to be used as a shield to protect our captors on their march into Ghent. I am not usually very particular as to what use I can make of myself, but the prospect of having the honour of leading the Huns did not appeal to me from any point of view. In fact, without any suggestion of untruthfulness, I may say that I thoroughly disliked the idea of being a human shield, for I knew how well the Belgians shot. However, there was a funny side to it, and once again I laughed with very nearly disastrous results.

Our hosts did not omit the customs of polite society for they sent an officer to bid us "good night" and "pleasant dreams." Translated, his words, or growls, were, "If any one of you speaks, gets up or moves you will ail be immediately shot." We replied with great politeness, "Good night," whereupon he glared at us most ferociously and growled some rude remarks which lacerated our feelings to such a degree that we could scarcely refrain from a burst of laughter. Fortunately, however, we did control our features, but we lamented the fact that the Germans are so entirely without humour.

That night was one that must live in my mind so long as I stay on this troublesome old earth. Picture the scene to yourself: a small group of closely - huddled - probably-going-to-be-shot human beings, very thoroughly surrounded by a portion of the magnificence of the great German army, all in full battle order. On our right a row of some fifteen burning cottages, the red glare from which painted everything in fantastic dancing patches of dull red. All was as quiet as the poor dead bodies that lay scattered along the road, staring with unseeing eyes at the starlit heavens. Behind us, beyond the groups of sleeping men and watching sentries, stood the remains of several corn stacks which had been torn apart to furnish bedding for the men (grain was not so valuable in those days, and wasteful destruction was the order of the day, - how little those devastators foresaw the time when food to them would be more precious than gold!). Beyond these rose the pale full moon, casting its cold indefinite coloured light on the objects surrounding us. The contrast of that cold light and the warm glow of the fires was wonderful and the bayonets gleamed now red and now white in the varying light. It was beautiful but it did not seem real. It was a stage setting such as one seldom sees in nature, and I longed to put it on canvas.

The dismal crackling of the burning timber, and the peaceful snoring of the tired troops, were the only sounds, save the occasional groans of one of the Belgians who lay next to me. The poor fellow was in terrible mental agony. He lay there never for a moment taking his eyes from the nearest cottage yet saying nothing but a muttered heartrending, "Mon Dieu, Mon Dieu," every now and then. What a long, long night that was and how busy our thoughts were. Among other things I wondered what would my wife and children say if they could see me? Would I see them again, and so my thoughts wandered between the short fitful dozes.

The air was very keen and I wrapped a copy of the *Times*, which I happened to have in my pockets, around my legs to keep out the cold wind. With the first glimpse of daylight I noticed that the headline across my knees, in large black type was, "German Atrocities in Belgium." That did not strike me as a healthy thing to display, so I quietly and unobtrusively buried it.

In the dim soft light of the early morning, when everything was painfully quiet, I noticed that my unhappy neighbour stared with renewed intensity. The horror and pain depicted in those eyes I shall never forget, and what was the cause of the increased agony? A small procession leading out from the nearest ruined cottage. Some black-robed priests were carrying five stretchers on each of which lay the remains of human beings, charred, distorted and so terribly still. The poor man broke down at the sight and bursting into bitter tears said:

"There goes my whole family. My mother, my wife and my three little children. Oh! Holy Mother of God, why don't they kill me too? I have nothing to live for."

This you may say is a small incident, but it is typical of what was happening all over Belgium and must surely call down the curse of the Almighty on those who are responsible for the uncalled-for misery and cruelty which characterised the invasion of unoffending Belgium.

* * * *

Thanks to a stroke of unexpected good fortune the following day saw us safely back in Ghent, but our troubles were not entirely past. It appeared that some Belgians had seen us going toward the German cavalry patrol, and had watched us go with them on the road to Melle. With some reason they concluded that we were spies, and it required a lot of explaining before we were freed from the suspicion. The fact that we had been living in a German-owned hotel, and had been taking our meals at a German restaurant did not help our cause. I need scarcely add that we had no idea of the nationality of these places, and thought they must be all right as they were allowed to do business in this important Belgian town.

Chapter II
Wounded at Alost

NOTHING WORTH REGARDING as of especial interest occurred during the next week or two so I made a trip home and stayed there three or four days in order that my family might see that I was still alive. Dame Fortune had been good to me, and I owed it to her, and incidentally to my wife, to be more careful in the future than I had been in the past and whatever happened not again to get caught by the Germans. It is all very well to play the fool occasionally - it keeps one's blood moving and prevents that terrible disease known as vegetating, but to make a practice of doing so is not entirely desirable, as the old Dame who takes care of fools, objects to working overtime and lets you down roughly when you least expect it.

For some days after my return from England nothing very exciting occurred. There had been some minor engagements and skirmishes in the neighbourhood during which a few peasants had been killed and a number of farmhouses burned.

We had experienced a few hours of interest when out in search of a certain hospital in which, I had been told, a brother of mine lay wounded. His death had been reported at home, but there seemed room for considerable doubt, and believing that all reports following the battle of Mons must necessarily be more or less unreliable, I had followed various clues, one of which was that he had been wounded and was still in Belgium. The place was a fair distance from Ghent, so I engaged a large motor and a driver who knew the country. As we proceeded on our way, disturbing rumours of raiding Uhlans being in the immediate vicinity continued to reach us. Added to this our car proved to have very defective tyres and, as if this was not enough, the weather became very unruly. The wind increased to a gale and flurries of rain proclaimed themselves the advance party of a regular downpour. Stopping at a fair sized village we made enquiries regarding the hospital we were in search of, and learned that it had been completely abandoned. This was very unsatisfactory and left us no alternative but to turn back with the hope of reaching Ghent that night.

That was a run to be remembered. Tyre after tyre burst, while the rain came down in torrents. Finally when still some miles from Ghent the chauffeur announced that he could go no further. The last tyre had a bad blowout and we had no more repair material, in other words we were done. Now of course this should have been the moment for the Uhlans to appear, but good luck had not altogether abandoned us and they did not arrive. We pushed the car to the side of the road and abandoned it, and after searching for some time managed to find a man who had a carriage of sorts and so, dripping wet, very tired, and a little bit discouraged, we got back to Ghent late that night.

During these weeks at Ghent there was a steady stream of refugees from the stricken areas. People of all classes driven from their homes by the ruthless Huns. Many of these unfortunates had terrible stories to tell. Some had lost their children and they told how the poor little innocent victims had been carried on bayonets by the savage brutes of soldiers. Others gave ghastly accounts of how the wretched women had been maltreated, how some had had their breasts cut off and nailed to the doors, as a warning of what would happen to any who dared oppose the will of the invader. Others had been violated in the most brutal manner with every imaginable refinement of torture. It made one's heart ache to hear these fearful stories and to know that a great nation which had been considered civilised should stoop to such a barbarous means of terrorising a peaceful people whose only crime was their faithfulness to their own small and almost defenceless country. Some say that the behaviour of the troops was due to drink but the argument is bad, for the German soldier is so highly disciplined that he does not get drunk unless he is permitted as a part of a devilishly conceived plan. One cannot but believe that in many, if not most cases, the soldiers would have been loath to commit the atrocities had they not been inflamed by liquor, and there are some instances where they even refused to obey their officers and were shot because they could not bring themselves to go contrary to their better natures.

One day I met an English officer, Capt.——, who had been wounded at Mons and had, thanks to a kindly Belgian nurse, managed to make his escape from a temporary hospital. He told me that when he lay on the field badly wounded he saw a German army doctor or under-doctor examine an English sergeant who was shot through the leg. After binding up the leg wound the brute deliberately fired two revolver bullets through the man's shoulder, then strange as it may seem he bound up these fresh wounds and had the victim taken to a hospital. It happened that he and Capt.—— were put in the same room. The unfortunate sergeant died three days later. Surely no more cold-blooded murder could have been committed. Germany imagined at that time that she was bound to win, and therefore would not be called to account for her inhuman behaviour, and the violation of all the rules of modern warfare.

Toward the end of September there was some fairly heavy fighting not many miles from Ghent. Unfortunately we were prevented from getting to it thanks first to the unscrupulous conduct of a certain newspaper correspondent who by unfair means got possession of the car we had engaged. It was a great disappointment to us but we could do nothing except take a carriage which was a slow and very unsatisfactory substitute. However, with this we should have been able to accomplish something had not an American press man, who evidently feared we would steal his thunder, put a spoke in our wheel by telling some queer story to the officers who had their headquarters behind the firing line at a place which could not be passed without their sanction, and they absolutely refused to honour our passes. There was nothing for it but to return to Ghent, where thanks to the American Consul we managed to secure a good car and chauffeur for the following day, when we made an early start.

The fighting was on the road to Alost, at a village whose name I have forgotten. We were armed with valuable letters that would take us anywhere we wished to go. These and a lot of English illustrated papers (we bought up all the supply in Ghent) and plenty of cigarettes for presents did wonders and we met with no opposition. In fact, we were received with open arms.

A good share of the fighting was on, and near, the main road, so we were able to take the car right into the firing line. On our way we passed a long stream of refugees trudging with what they could carry toward Ghent. The peasants who were on the Belgian side of the fighting line were scarcely at all concerned, but continued their every day pursuits, totally disregarding the fire of artillery, rifle and machine guns. When a shell would tear a branch from a tree the thrifty people would immediately go after the branch and cut it up for firewood. Their coolness was remarkable.

It happened soon after we had reached the Belgians' advanced position that they decided to retire a few hundred yards to where their artillery would get a better field of fire on the slope of a low hill. As they turned on the road I managed to secure some cinema films of both their artillery and cavalry. Curiously enough they had no infantry further forward.

Having used up the spool of film that was in the camera I decided to reload before moving after the troops. This was rather unfortunate as it turned out, for the next minute the Germans opened up a steady rifle fire, all aimed apparently at the car which presumably they mistook for a machine-gun car. The first few shots went somewhat wild but soon they came unpleasantly close, and I thought it safer to complete the loading of the camera while sitting behind the row of trees which lined the ditch on the roadside. For nearly half an hour we were unable to make our departure as the bullets were cutting the bark about our heads. The Germans were only about 500 yards away and yet strange to say they never once hit the car. Nevertheless it was to say the least of it an awkward situation for us to be caught *between* the Belgian and German lines.

During a momentary lull in the firing we jumped into the car and with no regard to the speed laws made an ignominious retreat until we were well back of the Belgian front line. There was no object in remaining much longer as the fighting was dying down. On the whole the Germans had had the worst of it and had lost a fairly large number of men, many of the killed being men of considerable age with quite grey hair.

The next day, September 27th, we made an early start as we were told that there was every indication of severe fighting in or near Alost. Before we had gone more than eight or nine miles we met the sad procession of refugees which marks the German advance. For miles it was an almost unbroken line of men and women and children, some twenty thousand, all told, most of them walking, or rather struggling under immense burdens of household treasures, - a more extraordinary assortment of belongings could scarcely be imagined! The younger people seemed quite cheerful, but the old men and women, who hobbled along laboriously, were terribly downhearted, for well they realised what the exodus meant, and to be torn from the home you have known from infancy is a hard wrench, especially when it is practically certain that the home will be completely destroyed. No wonder then that they were sad and murmured bitter words against the heartless invaders. In the procession were some few carriages and carts piled high with everything from beds to pictures, from people too infirm to walk to tiny babies sleeping peacefully among the collection of household gods. Carts drawn by dogs were numerous, and some there were which combined horses and dogs for their motive power. On one side of the road this dreary line marched northward, many of them would ultimately reach the hospitable shores of England, the protector of small nations; while on the other side, going south towards the ever increasing booming of guns were the Belgian soldiers of all branches of the army, a cheerful lot who cracked jokes with the refugees and told them what they were going to do to the Germans. They were a strangely hopeful body of men who did not realise in any way what lay before them.

We passed one particularly jolly crowd and met the daredevil soldier who only a short time before had stolen a train from the Germans. He told us with a keen sense of humour how he had been out one day on a private sniping expedition, when he saw an empty train brought to a siding where there were a number of German troops. Being a locomotive engineer he conceived the bright idea of making off with the train. The Germans, entirely unsuspicious, left it quite unguarded, so he carefully crawled along the ditch and made his way to the engine and started it off. At first it did not occur to the Germans what was happening. Finally they realised that the train had been stolen, and they opened a perfectly harmless rifle fire. Thanks to our cheerful friend's knowledge of the lines he managed to return the train to its rightful owners, the Belgians.

It was late in the morning when finally we reached the outskirts of Alost, to find that there was considerable artillery activity going on. The Germans were using a few fairly large shells which they dropped about the town in a very aimless way. We could see no definite object in the attack except a sort of general idea of destruction, while the Belgians numbering in all apparently about 10,000 were trying to keep possession of the town. We paid our respects to the General commanding the operations and asked if we might go forward to where the fighting would be most active. I told him how anxious I was to get some moving pictures which would show our people how well the Belgians fought. He frankly expressed the opinion that I was, without any doubt, a lunatic (to which I readily agreed) and that if he gave me permission to go forward I should probably get killed and blame him. He smiled when I pointed out that I would positively undertake not to blame him in the event of my getting killed, and so he allowed us both to go forward.

The town of Alost was in a state of semi-desertion. The thousands of people we had passed on the way had simply closed their front doors. Here and there some more courageous souls remained in their homes, notwithstanding the warnings they had received from the troops. The streets were occupied by scattered lots of soldiers, and the occasional groups of civilians who waited, hoping that the Germans would be repelled, and they would be allowed to remain.

When we asked the way down to the street where the staff officers told us the fighting was most likely to take place, the people thought us mad and said we would surely be killed if we went there. However we finally reached the square and found it occupied by quite a fair number of troops, most of them dismounted lancers. There were also a few machine guns arranged to hold the various converging streets. Just what the Germans were doing, or trying to do, was difficult to understand. Occasionally the singing of a shell followed by terrific detonation disturbed the otherwise quiet of the day. These shells seemed to be fired simply at the town in general without any definite target. Some dropped in the homes for old women, others on buildings of no special value, all doing material damage, without gaining any military advantage beyond showing the citizens that it was wise to get out while yet they could.

After a talk with some Belgian officers we decided to go down toward the canal with a body of the dismounted lancers who were to hold the canal bridge. With them came two armoured machine-gun cars. The position chosen was a small street in which about fifty yards from the canal bridge a barricade (composed chiefly of barrels of fish) was hastily thrown across. Here the troops ensconced themselves, while I, selecting a suitable place which offered a good view, assembled my "movie" camera. Evidently the Germans saw it, and presumably mistaking it for a machine gun, began to be very disagreeable, firing a number of shrapnel shells. These all went wide of the mark and only occasional bullets fell near enough to be picked up as souvenirs. The Belgians called them "German hail," and were much amused at the poor shooting. We were laughing at it all when suddenly the keen whistle of a well-directed H. E. (high explosive) shell made us change our tune. That it was coming pretty straight there could be no doubt. There was equally no doubt as to the utter impossibility of doing any dodging. One's thoughts move quickly, and I remember as I stood flat against the door near which the camera was standing, wondering whether this was to be the end of my Belgian trip. The shell struck immediately over my head and I felt as though the end of the world had come. The deafening sound of the explosion, the falling of bricks and plaster and the choking sensation as the fumes and dust were swallowed was all very terrifying. The camera was falling and I instinctively grabbed at it. Then a sharp pain stung my leg and I thought it must be broken. But on kicking it about I found that there was nothing serious the matter, only a flesh wound.

The whole air seemed full of confusion, for several more shells were coming and it seemed as though I ought to be making photographs, so in spite of being rather stunned, and almost blinded, I took the camera to the other side of the street, and proceeded to turn the crank, and got a few feet of film, though I could not see what I was getting. The handle had only been turned a few times when in the midst of the turmoil I heard the Belgians retiring at the double, and with them came the snorting machine-gun cars. Retreating apparently was the fashionable form of amusement, so wishing to keep in the fashion, and not caring to be left alone, I also retreated, camera and all, and well it was that I did so for the next shell, a large one, landed within a few yards of where I had been standing. It would have very effectively cured my taste for adventure had I remained a few seconds longer. It is perhaps superfluous for me to say that I felt badly shaken and generally much the worse for wear. Yet fortunately I was able to keep going for some time and secured a few interesting films.

While in the town square, after the retreat from the canal, a party of Belgian cyclists volunteered to silence a certain German machine gun which was doing a lot of damage. They were given permission, and half an hour later returned, bringing with them the troublesome gun. To say they were delighted scarcely expresses it. It appears that they were residents of the town and knew intimately the building in which the gun had been hidden. By going through back lanes and cellars they had come on the gun crew quite noiselessly, and - well, anyway, they brought the gun back, and were none the worse for the experience. This I may say is very typical of the way in which the Belgian soldier likes to do things. He seems to like individual jobs, and can usually be relied upon to give a very good account of himself.

The rest of the events of that day were very indistinct and hazy in my mind. I can remember seeing black-robed priests walking and cycling into wherever the fighting was thickest and nuns, too, all bound on their errands of mercy, giving what aid they could to the wounded and dying, caring nothing for their own safety. Indeed, the unselfish work done by these good people throughout Belgium stands out with glorious clearness, and they sacrificed their lives without a murmur, satisfied only to be able to follow out the teachings of their sacred calling, to do whatever good lay in their power without thought for themselves.

This day at Alost was my last one in Belgium. The effect of the shell began to tell, and, realising that I was in for trouble, it seemed wise to make all haste for England. It was very hard luck having to give up just then, for only a day or two before I had succeeded in obtaining passes which would have allowed me to go to Antwerp and do photographic work during its bombardment, which unfortunately seemed so imminent. But perhaps it was all for the best that for two months I was laid up as a result of the overdose acquaintance with the high explosive, for the Antwerp show turned more disastrously than any one could have foreseen, and I might have found it difficult to get away. Still I remember how terribly disappointed I was when the doctor told me that Antwerp had fallen, and I was lying helpless in bed. Ghent, too, was in the hands of the Germans, and so was my "movie" camera which I had left in a small hotel. There was nothing to do but get well as soon as possible, so that I might join the army and pay back my debts to the Germans. Recovery occupied over two months, while the payment of the various debts will never be completely settled.

Chapter III
In England, From Civilian to Soldier

On December 14th, 1914, I paid my very first visit to that great institution the "War Office" and offered my services to my King and Country. Owing to the fact that I was about six years past the age limit my chances of being accepted were very small. But I assured the powers that were, that if they would not accept me when I made a truthful statement of my age I would visit a beauty parlour, have my face rejuvenated, and come back with a falsified age. After some consideration and taking into account the fact that I had lived outdoors all my life, hunting and studying wild animals in various parts of the world, I was sent down to be medically examined before a decision was made. The result of the said medical examination being quite satisfactory I was promised a commission as soon as I had gone through training in an O. T. C. (Officer's Training Corps). So far so good.

Next came the getting into the O. T. C. At first they ridiculed the idea on account of age, but after a little persuasion I got in. Shall I ever forget those months of training! Being completely ignorant of all drill the reader may well imagine what I went through. Whatever conceit had existed in my composition was totally and very thoroughly removed. I became the wormiest of worms, the kind that did not dare turn. I perspired, or I should say sweated (because only officers are allowed to perspire, privates sweat) out of sheer fright when I made glaring mistakes. At first we drilled in London (I was in the Inns of Court O. T. C. known as the "Devil's Own"), and were duly stared at by the ever curious and that of course made me extra nervous.

Then came the move to the camp out in the country and here the Regimental Sergeant Major, the terror of the "rooky," got in his very good work. He searched diligently for any traces of conceit in each one of us, and when he found it proceeded, with great gallantry and dash, to launch his attack. The result was withering. Some poor fellows fainted under the ordeal. Of course it was not long before I gave him an opportunity for personal remarks. I made a mistake, or to be more correct some one else made the mistake, and it placed me out of my proper position. Not being quick enough to grasp the situation I stood firm in a place where I should not have been. Suddenly six feet two inches (it looked like fifteen feet) of very straight Sergeant Major loomed up directly in front of me, and a voice like an ocean-going steamship foghorn belowed for the whole world to hear "You blithering idiot! What the H—— do you think you're doing, having your photograph taken?" etc., etc., etc., etc. He wanted me to answer him back when he would really and truly have laid me out, but I had not been born in the army, and had all my family in it, for nothing. With great bravery (for I was much too frightened to do anything else), I stood fast at rigid attention and stared, unseeing past the great man. What were my thoughts during this ordeal? My sense of humour was most dangerously tickled, and I had the utmost difficulty in keeping my face straight. What would have happened had I laughed, goodness only knows. But there I was, a man between forty and fifty years old, accustomed to being treated with respect, to governing instead of being governed, being "cussed" by a man who ordinarily would have had to say "sir" in speaking to me, and yet, was not this part of that great thing called discipline, the thing that is the keynote of a soldier's successful training, without which soldiers are little more than unruly mobs. All this passed through my mind as I accepted my "dressing down" and I felt not the slightest resentment.

For the time being I was IT while the other rookies smiled. But soon another fellow was attacked and he, foolishly, tried to exculpate himself, to explain how and why it was he had made a certain mistake. This was what the R. S. M. was looking for and he "did himself proud." The very earth shook with his roars as he explained with unwonted vigour what he and all other decent soldiers thought of the man who presumed to "answer back," and we all stood smartly to attention, the bitter winter wind nearly freezing us, while we tried our best to keep our faces from any indication of smiles. I may add that no one in that company ever again attempted to explain his mistakes to the K. S. M. on parade. Off parade we could be sure of a most kindly welcome. Advice and help were given generously, for he was a splendid fellow and he taught me very many valuable lessons.

For nearly three months I remained in the O. T. C. We started work each day long before dawn, when the roll was read out by the aid of an electric torch while we stood and shivered in the bitter cold, and woe betide the man who was late, and we worked all day. When we were not drilling, or attending lectures, or digging trenches, we were cleaning our boots or our rifles, for on each parade we had to appear smartly turned out, and as it rained every day except when it snowed, keeping ourselves and our rifles clean was not an easy task. Then we had those joyous "night opps" (night operations) when we fought very imaginary battles and marched very real miles, for the battle ground was always chosen as far away as possible from our billets, and we very seldom had the slightest idea of what we were supposed to be doing, while the question of who won was regarded as a strict military secret and under no condition was it allowed to leak out. Still I suppose it was all good training, it hardened us at any rate and that was very necessary.

There was one marvellous institution which always struck us as difficult of explanation. During that winter of '14-'15 a severe form of influenza was very prevalent. If any of us were not feeling well and had bad colds, in most cases the beginning of "flue," we were given L. D. (light duty), and this consisted of sitting in a bitterly cold and draughty lumber yard (where our mess and kitchen were situated) on the edge of a canal, while we fished icy cold potatoes out of tubs of icy cold water and peeled them with blunt knives. Now this did not in any instance cure the cold or intercept the "flue" strange though it may seem, and the net result was far from satisfactory.

My stay in the camp ended for me on March 15 when I received the glad news that I had been given a commission as a Lieutenant in the nth battalion of the King's Own Yorkshire Light Infantry, having jumped a grade on account of my age. Packing up was a quick job, and I was homeward bound within an hour after receiving the welcome news, feeling tremendously important, for was I not a real (though temporary) officer in his Majesty's Army? I was granted a few days' leave in order to get my uniform and kit (the uniform had been made for over a month and only needed the necessary regimental buttons and badges) and was as proud as a peacock of my new feathers, while my children were even more proud and took the utmost delight and satisfaction in seeing their father saluted. It was most amusing.

Then came the day when I joined my battalion. That was one of the greatest days of my life, one that will never be forgotten so long as I live. As I look back at all that has passed, and think of the delightful lot of fellows that were my companions for so many months, and now, how few of them remain! The years of war have thinned their number most pitifully. Every one has been in the casualty list, and some have been wounded several different times. No better lot of fellows had any battalion. We were like a huge family, working, studying, playing, and living together, with the one object in view, and that object is not yet attained.

It is perhaps unnecessary to go into any details of my life in England. Of how I first tried to move a company the day after I joined, as the company commander was otherwise engaged. The agonies I went through. The dread of the first General's review, in fact of all the things which every new and imperfectly trained officer must go through. Yet with it all I look back to the months of training as some of the happiest in my whole life. There was the great satisfaction of seeing the men develop; when I first saw them they were in any sort of clothes, without rifles or equipment. Then came the great day when the khaki uniform arrived, followed soon by the leather equipment, and the consequent difficulties of assembling the endless parts, and then rifles to take the place of the soulless dummies, and the men felt that they were really soldiers and we were, oh, so proud of them! Each march through the town in which we were billeted was a sort of triumphal procession.

Our Colonel, who fortunately was a regular, took the greatest pride in the battalion, and instilled in every one the keenest sense of pride and respect, and the battalion increased in smartness and efficiency in a most gratifying way. Our life was a thoroughly happy one, for with scarcely an exception we all pulled together. My own position was in a way rather curious as the Captain, who was second in command of our company, was a fellow considerably less than half my own age. A splendid chap in every way under whom it was a pleasure to serve. He knew more than I of matters military and so it was but right that he should have rank senior to mine. In our army we do not feel that rank must be according to age, we have many second lieutenants who are forty or even forty-five years of age and who do not feel that it is beneath their dignity to take orders from men very many years their junior. It is all a part of the discipline which is such a splendid thing for us all, both young and old.

Our life during the period of training was one of constant activity. We all had to learn from the very beginning what was necessary for the making of soldiers. In less than a year we must be converted from peaceful citizens, enjoying the privileges and luxury of civilian life, to well-disciplined fighting machines, and modern warfare calls for such a vast amount of technical knowledge that every minute of our time was thoroughly occupied. Fortunately the enthusiasm of our men was wonderful. Not only would they do what work was demanded of them, but on Saturday afternoons and Sundays, when they could have rested, they would ask us to give them special instructions. It was indeed a pleasure and a privilege to help to the utmost of our power. The days seemed only too short for us to do what we wanted yet we worked frequently from 6 A.M., our first parade for physical training, till midnight or later. The Huns might speak of us as an untrained rabble, but we were determined to show them that when we took to the field, be it in France or elsewhere, we should be able to demonstrate that even the untrained British rabble was equal, if not superior, to the highly trained German troops, born and educated to the one idea of fighting. Looking back at events after these more than three years we cannot but feel a thrill of pride at the way our men have behaved in the greatest war that has ever been fought for right against wrong.

In June of 1915, owing to appendicitis I was forced to undergo an operation and had the bad luck to be laid up for over two months. Hearing from our Colonel that the battalion would soon be leaving for abroad I rejoined before properly regaining my strength, which resulted in my having a breakdown, and I was not allowed to accompany them when in September they left for France. It was a bitter night for me as I bid good-bye to the fellows and saw them march off in a dense fog shortly after midnight. Not to be going with them was one of the greatest dis- appointments of my life and I was left behind to clear up camp (I. C. details was the name of my job). How utterly dreary and deserted it was! The endless empty huts, the silent mess, which so recently had been ringing with song and laughter of the fellows who were so keen to get into the fight, and now they had gone!

After clearing up the camp I was laid up till December, when I joined the reserve battalion stationed in the Midlands and remained with it until March when the Medical Board (after strong persuasive arguments and appeals) passed me fit for G. S. (General Service). Needless to say I was delighted and immediately applied for embarkation leave of four days, and within a week was on my way to "Somewhere in France."

We were a jolly crowd of some hundreds of officers, all bound to various units, and all in the highest spirits. Nearly all had friends or relatives to see them off, and it was interesting to watch the heroic efforts of the women, wives, mothers, children and sweethearts to keep smiling when one knew how very near the tears were. But crying in public is not considered the proper thing for our women, and least of all when seeing their men going to war. Dry, or almost dry eyes and smiling faces were the rule. Yet one wondered what would happen when the excitement of the departure had passed, when that crowd scattered and returned to their homes. They were proud to have their men go to fight for the country. Not for worlds would they have had them stay behind and seek soft jobs in England. Yet the dread of the future must have been hard to face. With none of the excitement which keeps the men at the front busy and cheerful, and prevents too much thinking, the woman has the harder task, the terrible task of waiting, waiting and always dreading the arrival of the fatal telegram which to so many means the end of all that they have held most dear.

As the clock struck the hour the long crowded train started. Every window blocked by weather-browned faces anxious for the very last glimpse of the waving mass on the platform, and soon London was a thing of the past, a grey smoky blur. We settled ourselves down for the journey, and for a time a strange quiet prevailed. Men were actually thinking, yet no one would have dared discuss his thoughts. Gradually conversation began, began as usual with the lighting of cigarettes. What a strangely sociable little friend is the cigarette. It breaks the ice of reserve among men as nothing else does and leads to the forming of many a friendship.

PART II

Chapter IV
Rejoining My Battalion

OUR TRIP TO France was entirely uneventful and on landing at B—— we all received our instructions. With several others of my regiment I was to leave that evening for the base, Étaples, commonly known to Tommy Atkins as "Eat Apples," and we arrived in due course in the midst of a howling snowstorm. Guides met us and took us and our kits to our respective tents in which we were soon packed like sardines. Each man had his "flea bag" (sleeping bag of blanket with waterproof canvas cover properly known as a valise). In the morning after overcoming certain difficulties in the way of shaving, etc., we reported to the adjutant, a delightful fellow who gave us our instructions. We were to draw "iron rations" (tinned beef, dry biscuits, marmalade, and a tin containing tea, sugar, and a cube of beef extract), gas helmets, field-dressing outfit, and sundry other articles considered necessary for the welfare of the soldier, and the following day entrained for the Front.

To my great delight I found myself bound for my old battalion. That was indeed a relief and a piece of extraordinary good luck. To have gone among a lot of strangers would have been hard to say the least of it.

The train journey was slow and rather uninteresting. On our way we stopped for a few hours at a fair-sized town where, after some difficulty, we managed to secure a bath, of sorts. The French people have discovered that we are a very dirty race, and therefore need a great deal of washing, so a few wide-awake ones have bought large tubs, or even baths, and arranged for a limited, strictly limited I might say, supply of hot water, and for the sum of two francs or so we are allowed to disport ourselves more or less according to our national custom. Privacy is not included in the agreement and while we, perhaps half a dozen to a room, remove the dust of travel, Madame and her husband come in and out and keep us supplied with water and towels. It is all a trifle primitive, but better than nothing. Following the bath, a fair dinner, with abundance of *vin ordinaire* put us all in good humour and we resumed our journey arriving at B——l before midniglit. The battalion was in "country" billets a few miles away, so we put up at the hotel and in the morning found the mess cart awaiting us.

It was delightful getting back to the old lot. Of course many changes had taken place. They had been in the battle of Loos which had taken its toll, and the long winter months in the trenches had also taken a few. Still the regiment had been lucky and most of the old lot were there. It was like going home to see them all again. They all had had experience of war, while I was green, which made me feel very inferior. I was fortunate enough to be given a company immediately, and consequently was much pleased with life. Our billets were in farm houses of very unprepossessing appearance and most unsavoury odours. Does not Bairnsfather describe them as buildings surrounding a rectangular smell or words to that effect? Well, that just about fits it. Cleanliness was not, and in many instances the people were far from friendly. Notwithstanding the fact that they received good pay for all the wretched accommodation, they did nothing but grumble. The Battalion was resting, i.e., not in trenches, but busy with parades and exercises necessary for smartening up. I had a splendid lot of junior officers and our company mess was as jolly and harmonious as possible.

Within a few days we received orders to move, but there was no intimation as to what our destination would be. One cold morning before daylight we started on a march of about eight miles to the railroad. On arriving, there was a short delay and we entrained for the south, the men chiefly in freight cars, and the officers in first- and second-class carriages. All day we moved along in a most aggravatingly slow way, finally detraining shortly before dusk not far from Amiens. We were all tired and dirty, and the men badly in need of tea, so as soon as the camp cookers were unloaded, preparations were made for a hot meal before proceeding on the next stage of our journey, about thirteen miles of marching.

As darkness set in, the sky to the east reflected the warm glow of the guns and the cold silver colour of the star shells, and the low booming told us that we were not very far from the firing line. Those of us who had not been into battle began to realise what lay ahead of us, and we could not help feeling a certain queer tingling sensation at each burst of the ominous red light.

My own thought was that some poor fellows were probably being killed or wounded, and when we moved along to the cheery singing or whistling of the men, war seemed a strange thing, a thing of infinitely great contrasts, and such a foolish and inhuman way of settling the affairs of nations. Here we were a body of men all brought up to peaceful pursuits to whom the idea of killing our fellow beings or of allowing ourself to be killed had not come into our heads until a few months ago, and yet now we were like thousands of others marching along as cheerful as boys going on a picnic, when if we would but give thought we must know that this march was taking us one step nearer to that wonderfully terrible thing, the modern shell torn, gas swept, barb-wired battlefield. I have often wondered whether the average soldier does much thinking. Does he look ahead and analyse what is before him? I do not believe he does. He just plods along patiently, doing his allotted tasks, quite happy if his immediate body comforts are satisfied, and giving little or no thought to what fate may have in store. It is better so.

While tea was being served, the French girls did a thriving business with chocolate, and cakes of low quality and high price. Tommy Atkins seldom misses an opportunity of spending his very small amount of money and can never refuse to buy from the girls, no matter what their nationality.

Darkness set in before we were ready to move, and then followed a very dreary march to the village of La N——, which was some twelve miles behind the front line. We were all very tired before starting and it took a great deal of work to keep things going, and in spite of all we could do the singing slowly died down as mile after mile was passed. Toward eleven o'clock it seemed as though that march would never end; the men smiled sadly and unbelievingly when I told them we had only a mile and a half more to go; they were quite surprised to find half an hour later that I had really told them the truth. We entered the straggling village and were met by our billeting officer and the battalion interpreter who guided us to our various quarters.

After seeing that my company was properly housed in a couple of very airy barns, I joined the other officers and we went to our billets and met a delightful welcome from a couple of elderly French women who insisted on giving us bowls of black coffee with rolls and eggs. These people were quite a different type from those we had been staying with near the Flanders border, and we found everything as clean as possible and to our joy each of us officers had a separate bed with nice clean sheets, and as it was well after midnight, and we had been up since three o'clock, no time was lost in seeking the sleep we so greatly needed.

The following week we spent at the village doing a certain amount of training and attending to the men's equipment, special gas helmet instruction being given on account of the Germans' continually increasing use of this vile form of warfare. At the end of the week we moved forward to the village of B——e, which was only about six miles from the front. Owing to the limited accommodations we were closely crowded into our billets but still, as usual, managed to make the best of things, and soon settled down after the ordinary amount of grumbling. We were fortunate in having secured a most comfortable mess for the company officers, but it was too good to last. Some senior officers discovered our comfort and we were promptly evicted and had to put up with very inferior quarters.

It might perhaps be well to explain to the reader how we arrange things when we are stationed "Somewhere in France." The Brigade, consisting of four Battalions, usually moves from place to place as a unit, but in order to allow for the separate disposition of the component parts, each company is made a complete unit which can be sent away without interfering in any way with other arrangements. This means that the officers of each company run their own mess, one of their numbers (and there are usually five and sometimes six officers) acts as mess president and he takes charge of accounts and buys all the things necessary, pays for the room, and every week a settlement is made, the total expenditure being divided equally. The officers receive the same rations as the men and supplement this good, though somewhat unvaried, diet with such luxuries as eggs, fresh butter, fruit, coffee and whatever liquid refreshment is procurable.

Each mess has its inevitable gramophone and receives its newspapers both daily and weekly illustrated, and is in a way a miniature club. As regards the men the organisation is not very different from what it is at home except that the sergeants are not always able to have their own mess, though occasionally they manage to arrange this with more or less satisfactory results. Each company is supposed to have its own travelling cooker, and this usually stays with the company, except of course during the time we are in the trenches, when it stays in some reasonably safe place as close to the line as possible, and the cooked food is sent up to the men by specially detailed ration parties.

At each village where any number of troops are quartered there is usually a Y. M. C. A. hut, or a converted barn, and this is a veritable godsend to the men, where free stationery is furnished so that letters may be written in comfort. It is their club. Games and music are arranged for whenever possible and supplies of the ordinary necessities and some modified luxuries may be bought by the men at reasonable prices. In every way these Y. M. C. A. places are of the greatest value and they should have the utmost support of all who have at heart the welfare of the men who are giving up everything in the way of homie, and home comforts, in order to do their share to free the world from the threatened tyranny of German domination. The only other place of amusement that is to be found in our billeting areas is the "theatre," usually a large barn in which a rude stage is erected with very much home-made scenery and settings. In these theatres both plays and motion pictures are shown, and the diversion is most excellent as it takes the men's minds away from the everlasting military work and thought. The plays are given by amateurs or ex-professional men in khaki, and by kind-hearted theatrical people, men, who for some reason cannot get into the army, and women, who volunteer their services as a contribution toward the welfare of the men who need healthy amusement just as they need food and clothing. The theatres are to be found well within the zone of fire though seldom nearer than three or four miles from the actual front line trenches and it is not an uncommon thing to see a shell hole decorating the building in which the plays are given.

Chapter V
First View of the Trenches

WHILE AT B——e I made my first visit to the trenches with the three other company commanders. They had all seen a fair share of trench life and there was no novelty to them, but to me everything was new and of course most interesting. As the distance from B——e to where we were likely to be shelled was about six miles we made the journey on horseback in order to save time. Our way took us along the crowded dusty roads and through the one long street which comprised the village of M——e, where many of the houses were more or less destroyed by shells, and it struck me as strange that so many of the people continued to live in such unsafe quarters. From this village our way took us along a shell-marked road on the sides of which screens of burlap and brush were arranged to conceal the passing traffic from the eyes of the enemy.

Beyond the village everything was desolation, the roadside *estaminets*, where the peasants used to meet and take the mild drinks of the country, were now only masses of ruin; fields, formerly so well cultivated, were now barren wastes on which even weeds could scarcely grow. The trenches of the opposing sides were clearly visible as we rode forward, strange white chalk-edged lines on either side of No Man's Land. The day was unusually quiet and only an occasional burst of shell showed that the war was still on. Now and then a sniper's rifle would destroy the quiet with surprising suddenness. But the singing of the larks and the general air of peace and quiet were not at all what one would have expected to find. Here and there along the roadside often guarded by shrines and crucifixes from which gazed the agonised face of Christ we passed the graves of French soldiers who had given their lives for their glorious country, and on these mounds of earth lay faded flowers, while many of the graves were surmounted by a simple cross on which instead of the image of the crucified Christ hung the weather-beaten cap of the fallen man. Occasionally a khaki cap told us that one of our own men had been buried alongside of his French brother in arms and on the cross was written the simple yet eloquent inscription: "No. COO private S—— regiment. Killed in action, February 5, 19——."

On reaching the ruined village of Bécordel we dismounted and left the horses in charge of a groom while we proceeded on our way to the front line. The first half-mile was through the communication trenches, irregular, narrow, zigzag ways which led us to the main system of the firing line. We had been given a guide at the Battalion headquarters and he took us to the various company dugouts along the line. These were simple affairs lacking in most of the ordinary requirements considered necessary for comfort. A rough table usually occupied the greater part of the excavation in addition to which there was something in the way of a seat or two. On beds composed of sandbags or ragged wire netting were sleeping officers who had been up all night and were now trying to snatch a wink of sleep. A guttering candle was the only form of illumination and it barely made the darkness visible. There were brief introductions to the sleepy inmates who immediately offered the inevitable cigarette without which in our life at the front no introduction seems quite complete.

The rough walls of the dugout were adorned by a few pictures from the illustrated papers. The usual selection being, one or two of the inimitable Bairnsfather cartoons and by way of contrast some of the coloured pictures of fair but not over-clothed damsels from *La Vie Parisienne*.

After a brief talk with the fellows the company commander, who was a second Lieutenant, offered to take us out and show the line. He did it most cheerfully for our coming meant that he was to be relieved within a few hours and that is an event of considerable moment to those who occupy the first line. For obvious reasons it is not advisable to have detail maps of the trenches, as there is always the possibility of the Germans making a raid, and the capturing of a map would be most undesirable. The trenches being somewhat complicated it was necessary that we should take very careful, mental notes of everything, and it was surprising how many things had to be noted. To me, unaccustomed to trenches as I was, it seemed a most difficult task to obtain and memorise a correct and adequate picture of the whole system. Especially as few of the trenches had names on them. The lack of signs seemed almost inexcusable and I determined that the first thing I would do on "taking over" would be to put some sort of sign-board in every corner in order to avoid confusion.

We found the trenches in fair condition though in places there were stretches of badly demolished line, certain spots were shelled regularly our guide told us and they had given up in despair all attempts at repairs. Each time they had tried to rebuild these places the enemy had interrupted the work after an hour or so by vigorous *strafing*, which resulted in many casualties. While crossing these danger zones we had to crawl to avoid being seen by the ever watchful German sniper. For the most part the trenches were fairly dry and the bottoms covered with "duck boards," i.e., wooden grills, much like the wooden "sidewalks" so often seen in some parts of America. These prevent the bottom of the trench from being worn by the constant traffic and enable one to walk dry shod during moderately rainy weather. The wet chalk or clay makes these boards very slippery so that walking is almost impossible without hob-nailed boots, especially for men carrying heavy loads.

Needless to say the extraordinary regularity which characterises the practice trenches at home was entirely lacking. The size of the bays and traverses varied according to conditions. The depth alone remaining fairly constant. In most parts the sides were sand-bagged from the bottom up to the parapet, in others wire netting, wooden or iron stakes or corrugated iron sheathing were used to support the sides. Dugouts of many sizes and in various degrees of decrepitude were located at more or less convenient places, but there had been no effort to make them either comfortable or even reasonably safe. How different they were from those built by the Germans, as we were to discover before many months. The contrast between the two was a proof of the difference in the points of view. Our dugouts were of the crudest possible type. They showed that we evidently had no intention of staying in the neighbourhood, while the wonderfully elaborate ones made by the Germans seemed to show that they expected to remain indefinitely. I might even say for the rest of their natural lives, for that was to be the fate of so many of them.

One was struck by the cleanliness of the trenches. No litter or refuse of any kind is allowed, and all the sanitary arrangements were thoroughly satisfactory. This is one of the great secrets of the remarkable health of our troops. The trenches being actually healthier than billets except during severe *strafing* and very wet weather. The things that made perhaps the greatest impression on me not only on this first visit to the front line, but also later on, was the *seeming* scarcity of men, the apathy and boredom, and the apparent lack of *appearance* of readiness. Here and there one saw a khaki-clad figure huddled under a ground cloth, looking for all the world as though he were dead as he lay on the fire-step or in some nook. In all cases such men are fully equipped and are never allowed to be separated from their rifle.

Occasionally one came upon an industrious fellow polishing his rifle or even shaving, or what was still more frequent, writing letters home, for that is the great recreation of the men. Here and there a sentry would be found peering through a peep-hole or gazing into a home-made periscope. Unfortunately regular periscopes were only too rare and sticking one's head over the parapet is not a desirable form of amusement unless one wants to stay permanently in France. So the men showed a considerable degree of ingenuity in converting small shaving mirrors into periscopes. They were usually attached to the bayonet, the edge being held toward the enemy, so that it was scarcely visible. Any object that can be seen is immediately and very persistently used as a target by the snipers. This leads to a highly praiseworthy effort on the part of every one to be as inconspicuous as possible.

I was very much interested in what I saw of the crudeness of our methods of firing rifle grenades. At this time we did not take these weapons seriously, notwithstanding the remarkable efficiency shown by the Huns in using them. Not alone did they send over immense numbers of the deadly grenades, but they fired them with painful accuracy. I noticed a couple of men with rifles that were clumsily fastened to stakes, to the triggers were attached pieces of string, then the grenades were put into the rifle, which was loaded with a blank cartridge and the men walked behind the nearest traverse for shelter in case the rifles exploded. Just as the two men I was watching were about to fire, one remarked, "Wait a minute. Bill, you'll hit the bloomin' parapet," so Bill returned to the improvised rifle stand and gave the rifle butts a shove down and then looked along the barrels to see that the parapet did not obstruct the free flight of the grenade. Having satisfied himself on this point he again sought the protection of the traverse and pulled the strings. After allowing a reasonable time for the grenades to reach their destination both Bill and his mate looked over the top to see what they had hit. One grenade dropped fully fifty yards short of the enemy trenches and the other a little nearer, but both were utterly useless. I did not wait to see what happened next, but the whole method or rather lack of method struck me as painfully bad, and a waste of grenades, which at that time were very scarce.

In front of our trenches there was a very irregular amount of barbed-wire, scarcely enough to offer any effective protection against an attack. While the German lines were most elaborately protected by great quantities of very heavy wire. More particularly was this noticeable in front of the second and third line of trenches. The distance between our line and the Germans varied from about fifty to two hundred yards. The nearest part being in the neighbourhood of the Tambour where a great amount of mining and counter-mining was being done. The net result of this form of warfare seemed negative. Neither side gained appreciable advantage, but so long as one side indulged in the pleasant pastime of trying to blow up the other side, it is obvious that both had to play the same game, only we tried to do our work a little better than the Germans and, be it said to our credit, our mines in nearly every instance were fired first, and that is a great and very important detail.

The entire ground between the lines at this point was a mass of torn chalky earth and deep irregular craters - a truly ghastly confusion.

Winding its erratic way among the craters hastily constructed barbed-wire entanglements were visible, and on these hung several human bodies. Their tattered clothing blowing in the breeze gave the effect of scarecrows, the gruesome scarecrows of war.

For the greater part No Man's Land was a desolate waste, pock-marked here and there with shell holes, a dreary uninviting tract over which the bullets of rifle and machine guns screamed all night and the sky larks sang during the comparative quiet of the day.

To the East beyond the many lines of chalk-rimmed trenches lay Fricourt nestling against the small woods, which were beginning to show the faint delicate green of early spring. The village was fairly intact and seemed strangely peaceful, yet in reality it was neither more nor less than a fort. Everything that modern military science could accomplish had been done to render the place impregnable. Its snug homelike red brick cottages were bristling with machine guns and its streets covered a veritable labyrinth of underground passages and immense dugouts in which thousands of troops could be assembled in comparative safety from our guns.

Our guide took us through his entire lines and then handed us over to the officers of the adjoining Battalion. They in turn showed us their trenches, and after an hour or two we returned to where our horses had been left, and made our way back to billets.

Chapter VI
At Bécordel - Strafed

TWO DAYS LATER we received orders to move forward. The Brigade was divided so as to hold the various integral parts of our front, and it fell to my lot in conjunction with another company to take up our position at the little village of Bécordel, which was about fifteen hundred yards from the front line, and from which we could see our own and the German trenches quite clearly. The village was badly dilapidated. The church and many of the houses were completely wrecked, but here and there a building remained in fair condition except for occasional holes in the walls or roof. The Germans seem to think that we Britishers need a lot of fresh air, and as soon as they know we are occupying any particular billet, they promptly proceed to ventilate the rooms by means of shell holes.

We found the fellows who were holding the village exceedingly pleased at the immediate prospect of being relieved. It appeared that every day the Huns had indulged in a "hate hour" and the shells dropped into the place in a most promiscuous and highly unpleasant fashion. The result was that there had been many casualties. This of course was most reassuring and comforting, for we had a spell of ten days still before us. However, there was no use in worrying and after we had bid good-bye to the relieved companies (*relieved* is a word full of meaning in such cases) we began to make ourselves at home, picked out more or less suitable places for sleeping and messing and saw that the men were properly housed. Then instructions were issued for protection in case of shelling, dugouts and cellars allotted to each platoon, and rough plans made in case of attack. The village was a very small one built roughly in the form of a T with an open square at the junction of the lines; at the side furthest from the front line trenches there was a small field more or less protected from the

Germans' view by two large barns whose roofs had been riddled by shell and shot.

As soon as the men had been dismissed they started the inevitable game of football in the small field. Everything was going smoothly when one foolish chap kicked the ball high. Apparently the Huns saw it. Now if there is one thing they hate besides a Britisher and an American it is football. This hatred dates from the time at Loos when the Irish regiment dribbled a ball across the line toward their trenches, as one fellow would fall another put the ball forward and this showed a lack of respect for the Hun. Such an attitude is disliked by the noble creature and to know that we contemptible Britishers were daring to play the game within sight of his trenches was insulting and he forthwith proceeded to stop it by firing a few shells. The men were promptly ordered into shelter and I then started across the square to see to the safety of the rest of my men who were on the further side of the village; fortunately for me I am a slow runner, for I had only taken a few steps when I heard the whistling of a shell. Needless to say, I stopped, stopped very suddenly as the shell struck just where I would have been had I been a fast runner. Had we coincided I feel convinced that the shell would have had the best of it, as it was I turned and made what I am sure was a speed record in my endeavour to reach a place of safety in a nearby cellar.

The following day passed without incident or shells, and we began to feel that the Hun frightfulness had been much exaggerated, so we settled down to enjoy a peaceful ten days in our little ruined village. It was not long, however, before our tranquillity was rudely disturbed. We were about to have our five o'clock tea in the open, outside of our improvised mess, when just as the tea was being poured a shell came screaming into the village followed quickly by another. This was most annoying as we had to retreat to the safety of the cellars and when the *strafing* had ceased our tea was quite cold. Fortunately no other damage had been done, except that a corner of our building had been shot away. That day our C. O. (commanding officer) paid us a visit and gave the order that the officers of our two companies must separate so as to avoid the risk of all of us being knocked out at one time. Under no condition were we all to congregate in one place even for meals. This meant that we must have our meals in relays as there was only one room fit for a mess. A day or so later while the other company were having their meal I missed one of my junior officers. On investigation he was discovered sitting in the mess. I was in the act of telling him that this was contrary to orders when my remarks were emphasised by a shell tearing through our verandah, a curious coincidence which resulted in a race for the cellar; the speed with which we accomplished this act would have reflected great credit on a lot of agile rabbits getting into their burrows.

One of our tasks while in Bécordel was to furnish work parties to assist the tunnelling companies who were engaged in mining under the German lines. About half of our men had to go each night for this work, and most unpopular work it was, both for officers and men, especially during wet weather. The enemy knew exactly where our mine heads were situated and amused himself regularly each night by dropping shells and rifle grenades among the work parties. The previous occupants of our village had suffered heavy casualties in this way, so we were not surprised when during the following night work the officers reported several wounded and one killed. Later on when the men had finished their allotted task earlier than usual some of them were seized with the souvenir-hunting craze and crawled out in No Man's Land to look for unexploded grenades. Unfortunately they discovered a few and in coming through the narrow trench on their way back to the village one let his fall; it exploded and caused no less than ten casualties. This resulted in an order that under no condition was any man allowed to touch unexploded shells or grenades.

The following day two of the victims of this unfortunate tragedy were brought through the village for burial in the little cemetery nearby. It was the first time I had seen one of those pathetically simple funerals. The bodies were sewn up in Army blankets (which the Germans with their high degree of efficiency would have considered criminal waste) and borne on light two-wheeled stretcher carriers; there was no guard or firing party, no one but the Padre and the men who pushed the stretchers, and so they were taken to their last resting place over which two more small crosses would be added to the thousands, yes hundreds of thousands that will remain in France to mark England's dead, her part in the great sacrifice for the rights of humanity.

Many strange things happened during the night operations. I was told that on several occasions the Germans had sent a man over dressed in our uniform. The fellow would crawl along and watch his chance to join our work party, with them he would work until an hour or so before daylight and then vanish with complete lack of ostentation, probably carrying valuable information regarding our mining operation. Such a task certainly requires courage and no one could help admiring a man who would take the risks.

Each of our officers took turns in conducting the work parties, and my turn happened on a fine and fairly quiet night. After handing over my men to the various tasks allotted to them by the mining officer, I visited their dugout, had a bite of supper and then accepted the invitation to go down the shafts. These were about one hundred feet deep and we went down on rope ladders. I was glad that many years of my early life had been spent at sea as it made the ladder descent a *little* less unpleasant.

On arriving at the bottom, I was allowed to take one of the listening devices, a sort of microphone which was fastened in the ground. By listening carefully I could hear the Germans working at their mines, apparently very near. It was an uncanny, queer, and not at all pleasing sensation being down there in the dark damp hole listening to men working with the sole object of blowing you to pieces, and I could not help thinking of what would happen should they decide to set off their mines while I was down in the stuffy, heated and very cramped place.

To tell the truth I did not enjoy the experience and was only too glad when my guide had finished his inspection and suggested returning to the surface again, but my joy was short lived for on arriving at the top I found that I was expected to go down two more of the shafts. Pride alone prevented my saying that I had had quite enough to satisfy my curiosity, especially as I was being entertained by blood-curdling stories of how mines had been fired by the Huns at unexpected moments with horrible results to the wretched men who were working below.

In going along the trenches I noticed cages of canaries and thought how nice it was for the men to have their pets with them, they gave a sort of touch of home. I was however, surprised to learn that these birds are taken down the saps as a test of the purity of the air. If they die the men know that the air is foul and unfit for human beings to breath so the supply of fresh air sent down by the pumps must be increased immediately. Not so very home-like after all!

It appeared that when we first took over this part of the line, the Germans had the advantage in the mining, but that for some time past our fellows had gained in every point. We had found a way of ascertaining when the enemy intended to fire his charge and thereafter we invariably fired ours first, with results entirely satisfactory from our point of view. This underground form of fighting is one of the many strange and ghastly developments of modern warfare and perhaps none calls for a greater degree of nerve control. It is no wonder indeed that the men frequently break down under the long-continued strain of working in awkward, cramped positions, the terrible suspense, and the long hours spent in the foul air, and it is astonishing that human beings can be found who will volunteer for it, knowing well what hardships it entails.

Shortly before daylight appeared, I was told that the men had completed their tasks and that they had given entire satisfaction and only one had been wounded (they were nearly all miners and thoroughly understood everything connected with the work they had been doing), so we made our way out along the narrow crooked trenches and arrived at our village in good time for breakfast.

During the rest of our stay at Bécordel nothing of great importance occurred; as a rule we received about five shells each day just to relieve the monotony; strange to say we did not suffer a single casualty from these shells, and lost very few men among the nightly work parties. The only work of importance we had to do was the planning of an effective scheme of defence and construction of dugouts. How it was the Huns did not give us a thorough and effective bombardment I could not understand as they could very easily have wiped us out with a few large shells.

On the ninth day of our stay, officers from the relieving companies came to inspect the place. They had heard terrible stories of the village and were greatly relieved when told how we had fared, and returned to their billets very much pleased with the prospect of a pleasant stay in our mass of ruins. That night, shortly before the ration party arrived, as it always did about nine o'clock, the Huns sent an extra allowance of shells and two whiz-bangs (field artillery shells, so called because the whiz and the bang, that is to say the noise of the shell coming through the air, and the explosion are almost simultaneous: if you hear the "whiz" you are alive, if you do not you are likely to be dead) landed in the street exactly where the ration party usually stopped. When the party arrived we showed them the holes and it was surprising how quickly the rations were unloaded and the horses driven off at their utmost speed. They had not gone more than a few hundred yards when several shells dropped in their immediate vicinity, but fortunately caused no damage, and the sound of galloping horses caused a considerable amount of amusement among our fellows, who imagine that the transport men have far too easy a time and run little or no risk.

The next day we packed up our belongings and eagerly awaiting the arrival of the relief. They were not very punctual and it was late in the afternoon before they finally arrived so we lost no time in turning over the place to them, I regret to say they had very bad luck; within an hour after their arrival they were caught by some shells and lost several officers and a number of men. Their ill-fortune continued throughout their stay and they suffered unusually heavy losses both while working at night in the trenches and in the village itself. It is curious how luck, good or bad, seems to go with certain Battalions. For a long time past this lot had experienced nothing but ill fortune while we had earned the name of "God's own" for our exceptionally light casualties and general good luck. Later the tide turned against us and we suffered terrible losses.

The march back from Bécordel to our rest billets was made on one of the finest nights I can remember, a clear full moon lighted our road and every one was in the best of spirits; on the way we stopped at a place where the camp cookers awaited us, and had tea; it was like a regular picnic and then in the cool of the night we continued our way reaching our former billets at La N——e about midnight, all wholesomely tired and quite ready for a well-earned sleep.

The day following a spell in the front line is always more or less slack, a general cleaning up is necessary and there are no parades. As the baths would not be available for my company until the following day, I took the men to a little river not far from the village and allowed them to indulge in a swim. The British Tommy has a mania for washing, and one of our greatest troubles is to keep him from bathing in all sorts of places whether they are suitable or not. It is a good fault but causes a certain amount of worry and anxiety. I once found some of my men bathing in a large pool in which were numerous dead rats, and these rats were by no means recent. The excuse was that there was no other water available. The whole question of water supply is a very serious one and of course the drinking of any that has not been tested is absolutely prohibited and men are severely punished for violation of the order. Practically all the water issued to us is chlorinated which makes it safe but very nasty. However one gets used to anything, even the flavour of chloride of lime in tea, and this is a severe test of one's adaptability.

During our stay in La N——e we had to do a great deal of trench digging. Rest billets are so named because one gets everything *except* rest. It is always work and more work and the greatest ingenuity is displayed by those who arrange our itinerary in avoiding any blank periods; each hour is filled to its limit of sixty minutes, though we are never expected to work more than 24 hours per day. Of course it keeps us out of mischief and certainly does not hurt our health and there is not the least opportunity for getting soft.

The trench digging that we were ordered to do had a definite object, we had to reproduce the German trench system which lay in front of our line. Rumour had it that we were planning a great offensive along an extended front and that our division was to have the line opposite Fricourt, a charming spot which promised well in the way of excitement. No one knew when the offensive was to be undertaken but there was a great amount of suppressed excitement at the prospect of actually attacking the Hun seriously and on a long front, and the men worked with a considerable degree of enthusiasm. Of course we were not allowed to discuss the scheme, but naturally every one of us recognised the arrangement of the staked-out lines that we were digging. The plan was made from a large series of aeroplane photographs and was therefore fairly accurate, quite sufficiently so for our purpose.

Few people realise the amount of preparation that is necessary for a big offensive, the intricate detail is bewildering, nothing can be left to chance, from the important question of water supply at each stage of the advance, to the position of the ammunition reserves, the food, the surgical requirements, the number of men needed, and the placing of them, it is an endless chain of detail. There must be complete co-ordination of the various branches of the army, so that no unit shall fail. Not only is there the main plan for the attack which presumes more or less complete success, but alternative plans must be worked out with equal elaboration. Even the chance of failure must be most carefully considered and provided for. All of this is done by the Staff at G. H. Q., then each Division works out its own plans, each Brigade of each Division does the same, and again each Battalion and each company until finally minute orders are issued to each platoon, so that every man knows exactly what is expected of him. The trenches we had to dig were a small part of the preparations and were intended for use in instructing the Brigade. Over these trenches different schemes and formations for the attack were tried, until by repeated practice every one knew what he must do when the great attack was launched. The whole thing was extremely elaborate and very satisfactory.

The work, together with certain parades, occupied practically all our time and energy, and our ten days passed only too rapidly. At the end of the period we moved forward a few miles to the village of V——e, when for another ten days we were kept busy with various branches of training. These included demonstrations of liquid fire and gas, and I can safely say that no part of the training is so thoroughly disliked. It is bad enough to be forced to face these barbarous forms of warfare when actually fighting, but to enter a trench in cold blood and have liquid fire launched at the trench is, to put it mildly, very terrifying. We were using instruments which had been captured from the Germans; they consisted of reservoirs containing oil under high pressure; the man who carries the infernal machine directs the fire by means of a long nozzle which is pointed toward the enemy; as the oil is released by pressing a valve to which is arranged a fire jet it is ignited, and belches forth a veritable breath of hell with a deafening roar like Niagara Falls. Anything better calculated to strike terror into the heart of man would be difficult to imagine. Yet our men had to submit to this attack in order that they might realise how little danger there was if they knew how to act, the great precaution being the necessity of keeping as flat as possible in the bottom of the trench, as the fire does not fall.

On April 30, I received instructions to ride forward the following day with another of the company commanders to inspect the line of trenches that we were shortly to occupy; my line was to be the part adjoining the much dreaded Tambour so I looked forward to a very lively ten days as the Germans were particularly active on this section. Early in the morning we started and rode to within about three miles of the line and from there proceeded along the road on foot. We found that this road was subject to a certain amount of shelling and in several places, there were large holes, which testified to the accuracy of the enemy's shooting. On nearing the visit the enemy had been behaving badly and we were shown whole sections of trench that had been destroyed by shells. The occupying company had suffered a large number of casualties and had been unable to do much in the way of reconstruction. The company officer said that every time he had attempted repairs the work party had been shelled and that finally he had given it up in despair. I was naturally interested in his report and inquired as to his methods. He said they found that in every case the shelling would begin after the men had been working in one part for half an hour or more, so I determined to try very short shifts. That the trenches must be repaired was imperative, if we wished to live in any sort of comfort and safety. For in their present condition they were scarcely fit to be occupied.

It was late in the afternoon when we bid our hosts good-bye with the promise that we should arrive promptly at the appointed hour two days later, and arrangements were made for meeting the platoon guides at a suitable place. In this part of the line the reliefs were carried out in daylight; this is far more comfortable than when done at night, which is necessary in some sections. So far as comfort goes the night relieving has absolutely nothing to recommend it, but it has to be done when the opposing lines are divided by perhaps less than fifty yards.

In returning to M——e, where our horses had been left, we were told to avoid the road and follow a little gully near which a new communication trench was being dug in order that men could be moved forward with less risk. On either side of the gully we had a number of heavy batteries which the Germans were always trying to "find," i.e., hit.

As we made our way along several shells passed overhead singing their drooning song of death. Now and then they would fall in the fields on either side of us making a lot of unnecessary noise and sending great clouds of earth in the air. About a hundred and fifty yards away on our right I noticed a hare hopping along in a field apparently not realising that he was in a most unhealthy part of the world. Suddenly there was a tearing screaming sound and a shell landed not fifty feet away from the poor animal. For a moment he was stunned and probably wondered what sort of giant sportsmen were after him, and then in a most bewildered way he went round and round as hard as he could, gradually increasing the circle, when another shell came and sent up a shower of earth. I thought my little friend must have been killed, but as the air cleared I saw his white tail disappearing with commendable speed over the brow of the hill.

On reaching M——e we got our horses and started back but had scarcely gone halfway through the village when the gas gong sounded. The ominous warning sent men scurrying about and within a minute every one appeared in gas helmets; what a queer grotesque effect they presented, scarcely human! Being on horseback we thought we could avoid the gas by galloping, but before long the smell of the deadly fumes reached us and we had to put on our helmets. The fellow with me was only acting company commander and had no experience with horses;

riding was in fact a painful performance for him, especially if the animal went faster than a walk. He dismounted to adjust his helmet and forgot to retain hold of his horse and of course the beast went off, much to the fellow's astonishment. After some difficulty I recovered his mount for him and we proceeded along the road warning all transport of the gas. Horses were promptly unharnessed and taken back as fast as possible, for in those days the animals were not provided with the protection of gas helmets. This was my first experience of the much dreaded gas and I confess it scared me badly. By the time we had gone a few miles the air was practically clear of the poison as the wind had died down with the coming of evening.

Chapter VII
In the Front Line Trenches

TWO DAYS LATER we left billets at V——e and moved forward in the usual formation adopted near the front when the Battalions never move in the ordinary column of route. This makes such a conspicuous line that it is considered unsafe, so we move in platoons several hundred yards apart. The road was so filled with traffic of all sorts that we were forced to form "two deep" as there was not room to go in fours.

At the appointed hour we arrived at the place where our guides met us and each platoon was taken through the long irregular communication trench to its destination; as it reached the front line, the relieving and very much relieved platoon filed out from the opposite end and down the outward-bound trench. In company with the sergeant-major I took over all trench stores and signed the necessary documents and bid goodbye to the officer in charge, but not before he had given us the pleasant news that after I had left the previous day the enemy had been unusually active and had given them a very bad time killing and wounding a number of men and still further damaging the trenches. A corner about ten yards from the company dugout had been completely blown away and a man who was passing at the time had vanished, only one of his boots having been recovered. (Later we found one of his legs nearly a hundred yards away.) Naturally this did not fill us full of joy, and I own to a feeling closely akin to dislike for war in general and trench warfare in particular. It is one thing to run the chance of being killed while doing something that looks like fighting, but to be potted while quietly (?) holding a piece of trench is not exhilarating at all. One feels like a cornered rat.

My line of trench included a frontage of nearly three hundred yards; this gave a hundred yards to each of three platoons while the fourth was kept in reserve in the support line a hundred yards further back. From the condition of the trenches it was evident that the right sector which bordered on the Tambour was by far the hottest part, so I decided that those who held it should be relieved by the support platoon at the end of five days.

By the time the men had been assigned to their various posts the sun went down and soon after we indulged in the regular hours' stand-to. During this time, every one is on duty and the fire-step is manned. Nothing occurred to relieve the quiet of the evening except a volley of five rifle grenades which fortunately did no harm.

After dark the usual listening patrols were posted and then we settled down to the long dreary night of watching. These nights seem very long and very monotonous, each side fires a number of shots across No Man's Land, both with rifle and machine gun, this constant sharp punctuating of the stillness of night seems actually to add to the monotony. Each machine gun is supposed to fire about a thousand rounds in short volleys of ten or fifteen shots. The idea is to discourage the enemy from doing any prowling about near the waste of No Man's Land and prevent wiring parties from getting too much pleasure out of life. Star shells, or Verey-lights, are sent up with a frequency that is quite disconcerting if one happens to be doing any work outside of the parapet, and it is astonishing how conspicuous these cold blue lights make a man feel. Occasionally the Huns sent something over to remind us that they were not asleep, and the dull explosions of the bursting shells made the stillness which followed all the more noticeable.

At intervals during the night the company commander is supposed to go the round of his lines to see that everything is correct and the stumbling along the dark trenches, being challenged at every bay by the unseen figures, is most uncanny. Having heard that occasionally a German, dressed in our uniform, finds his way undetected into our trenches and goes along gathering what information he can, I had instructed our men to be extremely careful and let no man pass no matter what his rank might be until he was properly identified. This caution to the men led to a somewhat amusing incident a few nights later, but only by good luck was it amusing. It nearly ended seriously.

An officer of the tunneling company was coming to pay me a visit on his way to inspect certain saps at the left of my line. On coming round a traverse he was challenged suddenly. In reply he gave his name and business, but the sentry was not satisfied and insisted on a close examination. The officer stood still while the sentry with fixed bayonet approached to within a few feet and asked numerous questions, at the same time calling another man to his assistance. Fearing treachery the overzealous sentry kept his finger on the trigger of the rifle. Probably owing to nervous contraction of the finger the rifle went off unexpectedly, and the bullet passed unpleasantly close to the wretched officer's head. It is difficult to say who was the more surprised or frightened. The unfortunate sentry thought at first that he had killed the officer, but a vigorous torrent of colourful language convinced him that he had not added a name to the casualty list, and he was equally convinced as to the nationality of the almost-victim.

The officer came to my dugout and reported the matter and when I suggested bringing the man up for his behaviour he would not hear of it as it showed what he described as commendable alertness and thoroughness, the latter perhaps slightly overdone. Later, I interviewed the sentry who was in a state bordering on nervous collapse. He was quite surprised to find that no charge would be made. I was sorry that it was not a German who had come along instead of one of our own fellows.

During the night most of the men are allowed to rest unless assigned to special duty such as repair work, wiring or patrol. A certain number, one or two in each bay keep careful watch while the others sit about ready at all times for any emergency, none being allowed to enter dugouts or leave the immediate neighbourhood of their bay. In most of the bays there is a gas gong, usually an empty brass shell case, at the first suspicion of gas these gongs are sounded and as the signal goes along the line every man is ready with his protection helmet. When the wind is favourable it is of the utmost importance that extra lookouts be posted to watch for the poison. Any little mist drifting across No Man's Land is likely to be mistaken for gas and results frequently in the sounding of the alarm. Speed is so necessary that it is far better to err on the side of overcaution, at the same time it must be remembered that the gas alarm is likely to "put the wind up," i.e., give the men a scare, especially among new men, and so it is not advisable that it should be sounded without cause.

To avoid worrying about the direction of the wind, I made a very sensitive wind vane. This was attached to an old bayonet found in No Man's Land and placed outside my dugout in such a position that it was clearly visible. When the wind blew from the enemy we of course took extra precaution. It is interesting to note that in the way of wind the Almighty has arranged things in our favour notwithstanding the German boast of divine aid. Throughout the North Eastern part of France and Flanders the prevailing wind is more or less westerly. This means that we can employ gas more frequently than those who started the vile form of warfare. It is hard to understand how the Germans could have been so careless when they made their compact and goes to show how careful people should be.

The men are so accustomed to strange and brutal forms of German warfare that they imagine almost anything unusual is associated in some way with the enemy. An amusing example of this occurred one evening when an immense cloud of cockchafers (insects resembling the American June-bug, but rather larger) came to us from the German line. The men seeing the apparently endless mass of flying insects thought they were in for some new Hun horror and I had great difficulty in persuading them that it was a perfectly natural phenomenon, and that the insects were quite harmless. Although it is true that I had never seen the cockchafer in anything like the numbers that appeared. The noise they made falling on the wooden duckboards, scrambling over the loose chalk or hitting against our "tin hats" made the task of the listening-posts extremely difficult.

I did not attempt to have any repair work carried on the first night in the trenches as the men were very tired and we had no empty sand bags, so beyond sending out a listening patrol nothing was done. Immediately before daylight we had the customary one hour stand-to which passed as usual without much excitement, and then the men had their breakfasts, after which rifles were cleaned and inspected and those men not detailed for duties were allowed to get what sleep they could. As company commander I had to send in various reports and I came to the conclusion that though nominally permitted to sleep during the daytime the permission was somewhat of a joke owing to the almost hourly reports on such things as casualties, direction and force of wind, number of grenades, amount of ammunition and rockets and general altitude of the enemy, and how many and what kinds of shells, etc., he had presented to us and what we had returned.

In those days things were very one-sided. The Huns had apparently endless ammunition while we had very little. So our reports would read something like this. "Enemy fairly active, between 6.30 and 7.30 A.M. 25 shells landed on our support line from point X to Y also 45 rifle grenades, most of which fell near point W. From 8 A.M. till noon 30 shells and about 100 rifle grenades fell on line between Y and U. Trench badly damaged. We retaliated at 9.30 A.M. by firing 5, 5.4 shells at X 20d 7.2 and 15 rifle grenades distributed on enemy front line from X 20b 7.2 and X 26b 9.2." This is about as high a proportion as we could obtain and showed approximately our daily allowance, while the Germans would frequently give us twice or even three times the above number.

Besides the reports I had to send in requisitions for anything necessary. I mentioned my very keen desire for periscopes *every* day but up to the time of my leaving none appeared, so we had to manage with our home-made contrivances. I even suggested that if regular periscopes were not available I would greatly welcome penny mirrors for which I would gladly pay, but these are not part of government stores and so none came.

The mention of these reports brings to my memory a certain day when I felt that a little sleep was due; for some time there had been a rather undue amount of enemy activity, such activity interferes with sleep. So I determined to make up a little of the shortage. With this in view I made out my reports and arranged that they should be sent off at the proper hours, and that if anything occurred while I was asleep that would interfere with the accuracy of the said reports I was to be called. Then having persuaded most of the rats to leave the immediate vicinity of my sacred person I wrapped my mackintosh around me and went to my chicken-wire-and-sand-bag bed. Sleep was gradually coming, when with unpardonable rudeness and customary insistence the telephone called me, "Are you there?" said some one miles away. "Yes, unfortunately I am," said I in a very unfriendly way; "what's wanted?"

"Please send immediately the names of any men in your company who can play musical instruments and what instruments they can play," said the unsympathetic voice from the region of No-shells and Much-comfort.

"What for and who for?" said I with increasing and surprised indignation.

"The Divisional Band."

"Damn the band," said I in my haste and replaced the receiver with a slam.

Now who can say that I was not justified?

Imagine my going round to the wretched tired men and asking each one what instruments they played. Even the strictest discipline would not have prevented them from *wishing* me in some place in which only asbestos instruments could be safely used. I confess I felt thoroughly insubordinate.

I was much interested to notice that my dugout received each day a great amount of attention from German snipers. The shots always struck about the same spot which happened to be directly over my "bed"; besides the bullets a few rifle grenades were also dropped on the same place at odd moments. For a long time I was at a loss to understand why this should be, so one evening I crawled over the parapet and took a look at the sky line of my dugout as seen from the enemy point of view and discovered a small stake protruding about two feet above the earth work. This evidently was mistaken for a periscope, and was the target which attracted so much unwelcome attention; on removing it the firing ceased.

My dugout was a very primitive affair about ten feet square, and six feet high with the floor two feet or so below the level of the trench. The sides were of chalk, and the roof composed of corrugated iron, covered with an absurdly thin layer of chalk, loose and in sand bags; every time a shot struck anywhere near, the chalk would come rattling down, and when a shell exploded within a hundred yards it caused a regular avalanche; even the rats, which were very numerous, caused the chalk to fall so that sleeping was difficult. Speaking of rats they really were a great nuisance, their surprising boldness and persistence was extraordinary. Food was taken from the table without the slightest hesitation, even while we were there, and when it happened that we were called away during a meal, if we forgot to tell our servants[1] to keep guard, the food would completely disappear in an incredibly short time. Then, too, while sleeping, these pests, both rats and mice, were very annoying. Several men were quite badly bitten while asleep and incidentally I may add having the brutes run over one's body was somewhat trying.

The "furniture" of the dugout was of a thoroughly primitive description; it consisted simply of a sort of rough table, narrow and unsteady, over which was a rack for food. This was hung by wires so that the rats and mice could not get to it without doing acrobatic stunts, and fortunately only a few were experts in that line. Some ammunition boxes served as seats, and two tiers of bunks made of very ragged mesh wire completed the list. For illumination we had candles, but owing to the scarcity they had to be used sparingly. Our "mess" kitchen was a rough dugout less than fifty feet away in a direct line, but a couple of shells had wrought such havoc in the trench between the two dugouts, that it was necessary to make a wide *detour* in going from one to the other. The Huns seemed to know our meal times and

---

1. The word servant, according to the custom in the British Army, applies to our soldier servants who accompany the officer whereever he goes and takes care of his belongings in case he is wounded.

invariably selected the moment when our servants were bringing us food to drop a few of the cursed rifle grenades on or near the path, and it was quite amusing to hear the servants apologise for bringing a soup plate with scarcely a spoonful of soup left. A grenade having caused the man to start violently while he was carrying the plate. I will say one thing for our service, we usually got the food pretty hot as speed between dugouts was always considered desirable. Often the men came in at the double, this meant that a shell or grenade had been heard in the air. The result was a race, and frequently a wasteful distribution of food along the trench.

During the first few days I had done my shaving and washing at about eight o'clock in the morning, but the Huns latterly selected that hour for some grenade practice, so I had to change my plans. I strongly advise the use of safety razors for trench shaving, as sudden explosions are apt to cause a degree of jerkiness not at all conducive to comfort and good results when the ordinary razor is being used.

After the first night I started having the trenches repaired and parapets replaced, and by working according to the short term plan already mentioned a fair amount of work had been carried out with very few casualties. About twenty minutes was the limit of comparative safety.

On several occasions the working party had scarcely left the place before trouble would come, chiefly in the form of rifle grenades; these, though disastrous to men, do not damage the trenches, but sometimes heavy stuff was sent over and the new work would be completely destroyed; one piece of line I had repaired eight times and when we left, it was once more a mass of wreckage. Of course no work that showed against the sky-line could be attempted by daylight and even if done at night it was not desirable to make any conspicuous change or addition, for it always enjoyed a *strafing* as soon as the Huns discovered it.

An idea of the number of sand-bags required in order that the trenches be kept in fair condition may be gained from the fact that in my company line, which was between two and three hundred yards in length we used from 1500 to 2000 new sand-bags every ten days.

Allowing that even 1000 were used on the average it gives a total of about 70,000 per day for our entire line, or approximately 255,500,000 per year for repairs alone. This may not be very exact, as various parts of the line differ so greatly, still it gives some suggestion of the vast quantity of this one article of war material which is needed.

The trench leading to my dugout had been widened to such a degree by repeated shells that it no longer afforded adequate protection. Repairs were urgently needed if I wished to continue in occupation, so one fine day I ordered eight men to rebuild the sides that had fallen down. As soon as I had shown them exactly what was needed I went into my dugout to write out some reports; within five minutes a loud sharp explosion announced the arrival of a rifle grenade, following it came a cry of pain and I rushed out. The men had scattered immediately, according to instructions in such cases, but one poor chap lay on the ground badly wounded. Knowing full well that the Germans nearly always send a succession of not less than three or four grenades, I hastily gathered the man in my arms intending to carry him into the dugout, where he would be more or less out of danger. The ground was wet and very slippery, which added to my troubles and made the man seem unusually heavy. No sooner had I started to walk than the singing of a grenade warned me that I must hurry, but strange to say my feet seemed nailed to the ground, and I simply could not move, it was a case of undiluted terror, for I knew that the grenade was coming straight toward me. I was paralysed, and waited, expecting to be blown to bits the next instant. My body might save the already wounded man, but even that was doubtful, I wanted to drop the poor fellow but feared that he would object.

How long it took that wretched death-dealing instrument to fall! Thousands of things flashed through my mind during that time which was not of more than a few seconds' duration. Then at last it came whistling into the trench; striking barely three yards behind me. I waited - but nothing happened. I even turned to look at it, and could scarcely believe my eyes, for there it lay quiet and harmless on the ground. One look was enough. I moved - and moved quickly, into the dugout where

I dressed the man's wounds before sending him with two of the others who were slightly wounded to the dressing station.

The grenade was afterward brought to me, it was a "dud" and as usual proved to be one of those made before the war, as it bore the 1914 date. It is interesting to note that nearly all the rifle grenades we found on our front bore the date of 1914, and all had the solid copper bars which are the length of a rifle barrel and the same diameter as the bore.

This shows two things: first, that the Germans must have had an unheard-of quantity of these weapons, for on my own company front, which as already stated was between two and three hundred yards in length we received from 50 to 200 grenades each day; assuming that even 350 were fired at every mile of our line, it would mean that about 35,000 were used each day on the British front or perhaps 9,775,000 per year; and this was toward the end of the second year of the war. Second, that the Germans who were known to be short of copper had not removed the unnecessary copper bars, for which a substitute could have been used shows how busy they were.

Later on the repair work was resumed and finished in a few days without further mishap, though there were several narrow escapes and no one seemed particularly fascinated with the neighbourhood.

Up to this time I had never witnessed a regular bombardment, but on the sixth day of my spell in the trenches word came from H. Q. that at a certain hour the village of Fricourt was to be well *strafed*, I selected a good position from which to view the show and at the appointed moment it seemed as if hell were suddenly let loose. Countless numbers of projectiles, large and small, came screaming through the still air and in a second Fricourt was lighted by the red glow of the shells as they burst on every part of the wretched village (it was only occupied by the military, all civilians having been sent away many months before). The earth shook violently with the terrific explosions and the din was appalling. Never before have I seen a more wonderful sight, a more marvellous pyrotechnic display, and it gave our men immense satisfaction, for it showed that we at last had some shells to spare, so that the Huns were learning the delights of being thoroughly shelled. From the numerous signals they sent up, and the veritable rain of their machine-gun bullets that tore across No Man's Land, it was evident they expected we were going to make an immediate attack. However nothing was further from our minds. We were simply indulging in a little "Hate," and from the dilapidated appearance of Fricourt the following morning we could see that our gunners had done some very excellent shooting.

On the seventh day of our spell in the trenches I had a very fortunate escape while walking along on a tour of inspection. The enemy had been unusually active, plastering the line with all sorts of disagreeable things, but by dodging between the outbursts of fire I had gone most of the round untouched, though one of the men had been killed close by me. He was one of the best fellows in the company, always cheerful and the fun-maker of the lot; his death was a great blow to us all. I had just passed a long rather wide bay and was in the act of stooping to get under an artillery bridge which crossed the trench, when a grenade struck the edge of the parapet not three feet away from my head; the sound of the explosion at such close quarters was deafening and at first I felt sure I was killed, but fortunately for me the force of the burst passed immediately over my head. Had I been walking erect it would have finished my army career with extreme suddenness, but as it happened, thanks to the protection afforded by the "tin hat," the only result was that one side of my face was paralysed for a few days, and of course the shock made me feel pretty uncomfortable.

One of my duties was to observe whatever was possible of the enemy's activities and report the same. For several nights I had heard a considerable amount of horse and wagon traffic and a lot of talking; this always occurred in the same place and at about the same hour. I reported the facts and it was decided that a little *strafing* would be useful, so on a certain evening I was told to observe carefully the results of a "shoot" which would begin when I sent word of the sounds of wagons. At a few minutes to nine the clatter of vehicles sounded clearly in the stillness of the night, word to this effect was promptly telephoned, and almost immediately a regular tornado of shells flew overhead and burst along the road at the edge of Fricourt. For two or three minutes this continued then, as suddenly as it had begun, it stopped and the shrieks of men giving hurried orders and the bumping of hastily moving wagons sounded in place of the bursting shells. The wretched Germans evidently imagined that the bombardment had ceased, but after a wait of about a minute it was renewed with increased vigour, and continued for five or six minutes, after which it stopped, and not a sound could I hear, apparently the whole ration party had been wiped out which, from our point of view, was quite satisfactory.

The ten days in the trenches seemed never ending. The strain was monotonous and the impossibility of having a wash or changing clothes made life anything but a joy. The lack of sleep was trying, especially to one who could not snatch short naps when occasion offered. Almost the only pleasure was the daily or rather nightly arrival of mail. This was a Godsend. Among my letters I remember receiving one from a great friend in New York. It contained a detailed account of a fishing trip in a part of Newfoundland where I had enjoyed some glorious sport in the days before the war. It told of fine salmon being caught, of delightful camps on ground I knew so well, and I felt sick of war, more sick than ever before; what a contrast there was in the events spoken of in the letter to the terrible conditions in which we were taking part. The fishing seemed like a story of fairyland. I wondered what the future held in store for me, and I longed for the feel of rushing water, and the joy of fishing in the wonderful wild lands of the North.

Not only were there letters and daily papers from home but occasional packages, containing cake or "smokes." I had asked my various friends and relations to send cigarettes for my company, and when these arrived in the trenches they were more than welcome and it was a real pleasure to distribute them among the men. Each day we had the task of censoring the men's letters. I think there is no more hated duty than that. Still it is very necessary The letters are brought in to the company commander's dugout at a certain hour, and every one must be read, initialed, and then sealed. A few green envelopes are given to the men who want to write of private affairs, these are sealed and the man signs his name and number; affirming that the enclosed letter contains nothing liable to censorship.

A small percentage of these are opened by the censor at the base, and if any one is found to contain military or other information of a forbidden nature the writer is heavily punished and is not again allowed to have green envelopes. The officers are trusted more or less to keep their own letters within bounds, and they only have to put their name on the envelope, as with the men's green envelopes, a few are opened by the censor at the base.

On the evening of our ninth day we were warned to look out for a mine explosion at midnight. I had never seen one and was naturally very anxious to know what it was like; from stories I had read I imagined it would be a very spectacular show, so I waited patiently in a good position about six hundred yards from the Tambour which was the centre of the mining activity. The night was clear starlight without the slightest breeze, nothing disturbed the quiet except the inevitable pinging of bullets from machine guns. Suddenly just at the moment of midnight there was a strange rumbling of the ground, it seemed to rock and shiver; at the same time a curious light in the direction of the Tambour showed the ground to be heaving almost as though it were boiling and rising slowly to the accompaniment of a terrific booming sound. Then quietly the boiling ceased, and the ground settled in the centre of the area and left a huge crater. Scarcely had this happened when another mine was fired and it acted in the same strange way and in the cold glow of the Verey lights men could be seen hastily taking possession of one edge of the craters, and that was all, yet it represented perhaps months of work and many lives, besides tons of explosives. The show was over, and I returned to my dugout to find that the results of the explosions were only too evident - for everything that could be knocked down was distributed over the ground; a mixture of chalk, food, boards, books and other odds and ends; and among it all were several unexploded grenades which an enthusiastic subaltern had collected at various times and placed in a niche in the wall, fortunately instead of falling on hard ground they had landed on some rubber boots, otherwise they might have exploded with results exceedingly unsatisfactory to our dugout. These grenades had been a source of considerable anxiety to me as the subaltern had a most enquiring turn of mind and would bring all sorts of strange grenades and other implements of destruction into the dugout and amuse himself taking them to pieces. For my part I never could see anything even remotely amusing in the game and I finally had to suggest that grenade investigations would be much more popular if carried out in a more secluded place.

On May 11th the officers of the relieving battalion came to pay us a visit and look over the trenches, and I was glad to be able to show the amount of work that had been accomplished. We had used nearly two thousand new sand-bags in the work, as well as nearly a thousand filled ones taken from the mine saps, and with the exception of two short stretches toward the Tambour end the line was in very fair condition. The trenches had been made narrower and were there- fore very much safer, names had been put on each corner, in fact everything showed how much good work the men had done. In spite of the very considerable amount of shelling to which we were subjected every day our casualties were only about fifteen.

The following day we all got ready to leave, hours before it was necessary. We had had quite enough of the trenches for the present and were all anxious to enjoy a wash, and change our clothes. Some of the days had been very hot so we all suffered from swollen feet. In their de- light at the prospect of getting back to billets some of the fellows began to whistle cheerful tunes and though this was quickly stopped, the Germans evidently heard it and concluded that nothing but the immediate prospect of relief could make the men so light-hearted. The result was that they started a vigorous *strafe*. All sorts of stuff was sent over, shells, "minnies" and grenades, and one could scarcely go ten yards along any trench without finding pieces of newly fallen metal. Things looked very bad, and I was only too glad when at three-thirty the last of the relief arrived and I was able to hand over the responsibilities of holding this piece of the line and say good-bye to the extremely unhealthy neighbourhood and wish the new company commander the best of luck.

On reaching the outskirts of Bécordel I selected a quiet place which seemed well sheltered, in order to call the roll, as I feared the company had suffered heavily during the last two hours. No sooner were the men lined up than a fairly big shell came singing toward us. It looked bad for us all and I shouted to the men to lie down; before the words were out of my mouth the shell landed not thirty yards away in a small new cemetery, and it was followed by four others, all falling within an area of a few yards, *but not one exploded*. Such luck was really remarkable, but scarcely more so than the fact revealed by the roll call that not a man had been killed during the bombardment which had lasted about two hours while the relief was being carried out. Luck is a queer thing and our men began to think that Providence was especially kind to them, and they made the march to B——e in the best of spirits. We stayed there only for the night, and the next morning proceeded to La N——e, our favourite billets.

Chapter VIII
Preparing for the Great Offensive

On arriving at La N——e I was asked whether I would care to take charge of the Battalion scouts and undertake their training, as the General wished each battalion to have an officer and sixteen reliable men trained for this work. I was delighted to take over the task, and a few days later was appointed Brigade Scout & Intelligence Officer, an appointment which I most thoroughly appreciated, as it gave me opportunity to work out some novel schemes for training the sixty-four men and four officers in all the branches of scouting. As most of my life had been devoted to stalking wild animals the lessons I had learned proved of the greatest value. The men were wonderfully keen, they took to the work very readily and were as good a lot of men as I have ever known. I look back with utmost pleasure to the days spent with them. We worked very hard both by day and night and the men became so enthusiastic that they continued making and developing schemes even during their leisure hours.

Among the things I had to teach the scouts was how to take cover under all conditions and make the best of any situation. The men had no knowledge of the value of protective colouring, nor even knew there was such a thing, except two, one of whom had been a gamekeeper and the other a poacher; of these two the poacher was the better, he took to the work as naturally as a duck takes to water.

At first when the men were told to conceal themselves in woods or hedgerows, in a position which would enable them to see without being seen, they would invariably hide behind the thickest bush they could find and then break off any branches that happened to be in the way, with the result that gleaming white scars stood out with conspicuous clearness, advertising the man's position as surely as if he had hung out a white handkerchief.

In teaching, the best way is to let people make the mistake, point out how or why it is a mistake, then let them discover the remedy. This makes them understand what they are doing, and gives them a chance to think. When the men saw why they had been found, I let them have another try, this time instead of completely breaking the branches they did exactly as I expected, they bent down, or partly broke the branches, so that the under side of the leaves showed. Now every one who has taken the trouble to observe things outdoors will have seen that the under side of a leaf is very much lighter than the upper side; it shows almost white if placed against foliage in its ordinary position. The men were very much surprised to find themselves immediately discovered, and could scarcely believe that the upturned leaves had exposed their carefully selected hiding places. I then showed them how to turn this peculiarity of the leaves to advantage. In going through woods there is always the danger of losing one's way; under the ordinary conditions of life this may not be a very serious matter, but in the war game it may easily be a question of life or death, not alone for the one who makes the mistake but for many others as well. So I explained to the men how easy it was to mark one's trail by simply bending twigs so that the leaves will show their under-sides.

The objection to selecting a particularly dense bush was explained on the ground that the eye was naturally attracted to any object that stands out from its surroundings, as it increases the possibility of discovery however carefully one may be hidden. Even though one might not actually be seen, a chance shot might easily be fired just to make sure.

The great importance of keeping absolutely still, especially on days when there is no wind, was demonstrated by placing some men among the bushes, and telling them to move very slightly, while the other men looked on. The least movement of the leaves immediately caught the eye. I explained the disadvantage of keeping the head too close to the ground as in most instances it reduced the field of vision to such a degree that nothing could be seen more than a few feet away. The use of tufts of grass or leaves stuck into the clothes, in order to break the lines, was also explained with care, and the men soon realised how important it was to select the vegetation best suited to the surroundings, also the importance of not making the effect too solid.

In carrying out the work by practising under various conditions we had some amusing experiences, and in one instance narrowly escaped getting into trouble. I had divided the men into two groups, one lot were to conceal themselves so as to hold a certain line. The others had to advance without exposing themselves, and if possible creep through the line. If either side caught sight of a man, instead of firing a round of blank ammunition, he was to call out "dead," which meant the man was out of action. Of course the side that did not have to move had every advantage, yet it happened that they had the greater number of "casualties." The sides were then reversed with the same results. This was not very encouraging, as it showed that the men either did not keep sufficiently still or that they had not selected their places of concealment with care. In order to make them realise the great importance of carefully selected cover, and how greatly the advantage was with those who were holding the position, I picked out my best man, the poacher, and he and I arranged to take the same line which the others had failed to hold.

We were working in a valley which was more or less wooded and covered with patches of shrubbery. Immediately back of the line that we were to hold was a cottage, with the usual group of out-houses surrounding an ill-kept yard. Not having heard any sign of human beings in the neighbourhood I imagined the place to be uninhabited, otherwise I should not have chosen it.

After explaining to the men that we would stay within a certain limited area, less than a hundred yards in width and depth, I sent them off with instructions to advance at a given time. My poacher friend and I then proceeded to conceal ourselves with as much care as possible. The position we selected afforded an extensive field of view so that it would have been difficult for any one to have approached us unobserved.

In due course we saw evidence of the "enemy," here and there a bush would shake, very slightly it is true, but quite enough to indicate the presence of a moving body. Before long we succeeded in catching several of the advancing men, when a serious complication arose in the form of an old woman, the occupier of the adjacent cottage. It was most amusing to watch her as she moved about very cautiously and with every indication of suspicion in her manner, several times she passed within five or six feet of me, and of course I scarcely dared to breathe, the poacher who was about twenty yards away from me was so convulsed with merriment over the situation, especially when the old girl planted herself so close that I could have reached out my hand and touched her, that he nearly exploded.

Suddenly the storm burst as the woman caught sight of a khaki figure crawling stealthily among some underbrush; the stillness of the day was badly broken by a most wonderful flow of abusive language. Translated it meant, "Here, you dirty, crawling thief, you low-down pig, I see you; do you think you can come to a poor old woman's place and steal her chickens; come along out, oh! yes, I see you right enough (as the wretched fellow tried to make his escape unobserved); aye, and there's another one of you; come, I say, or I'll call my husband and he'll shoot the two of you, you miserable thieves," all this time she was getting more and more angry, while the poor men who could not understand a single word that was being hurled at them, did not know of what they were accused. For fear that the affair might end in trouble I finally stepped out from my place of concealment, to the very great surprise of the highly indignant woman and of the men, who had begun to think that I was lost.

I managed, after considerable difficulty, to explain that the men were entirely innocent of any thought of chicken stealing, and that I was simply teaching them to stalk the Boche. At first she looked somewhat incredulous, but when in reply to my blowing the whistle, men appeared as though by magic, from all sorts of places, the woman realised that it did not look so much like a chicken raid after all. She was most amused when I showed her where I had been hiding and explained how easily she could have been taken a prisoner.

Nothing would satisfy her but that we should come into her house and meet her husband. Under the circumstances we could not refuse, so we all trooped in, and were duly presented to the husband and his brother. I noticed that both bore the marks of war, one lacked an arm and the other a leg, which with considerable pride they hastened to explain was the result of the Battle of the Marne. They were both men well past middle age and were among that lot of marvellous men who had stemmed the impetuous onslaught of the army which the Kaiser believed would conquer not only France, but the whole world.

While our hostess told how she had caught us red-handed trying to steal her chickens and how we had sprung out of the ground and captured her instead of the chickens, all of which greatly amused the men, she was busy pouring out glasses of black coffee for all of us who cared to indulge; while we drank it she disappeared, but returned very shortly with a red plush album which contained photographs of her five sons, all in the army. With glistening eyes and a proud heart she told how three of them had died fighting for their country, while a fourth was in a hospital seriously wounded. Only one sound one left! What would she and her crippled husband do in their old age? The peasants depend so much on their children for support when they are too old to work that the loss of sons is a very serious misfortune; and yet when I suggested that we would all be glad to have the war end, she replied with extraordinary energy,

"We don't want even to talk about the war ending *until those German devils are beaten, beaten, beaten!*"

How I wish that some of those spineless creatures, called "Pacifists" could have heard that splendid French mother speak, she who had given so freely of her own flesh and blood, who had paid such a terrible price, who would lose, perhaps, her last son if the war continued and yet she wished, I should say, *demanded*, that there should be no question of peace without complete victory. Victory so complete that there shall be no possibility of the treacherous HUNS being in a position again to turn the world into a gigantic slaughter-house. When I told the men what the French woman had said they gave her three rousing cheers. Then all shook her toil- scarred hand; this was too much for her and she burst into a flood of tears, she wanted to embrace them all - her "brave children" she called them. After promising to return again soon and steal some more of her chickens we bid the kind people good-bye and left, all feeling the better for the encounter. It had done a great deal to make the men understand the spirit that was driving the French nation to such wonderful deeds of heroism.

As we moved off I drew the men's attention to the fact that they had been discovered by a woman while they were supposed to have been very carefully concealed. Also that I had caught sight of many of them, and that none of them had seen either the poacher or me. This was during the early stages of the training. They profited by each mistake, and soon developed extraordinary proficiency in their work. Sometimes I would send half of the party ahead, giving them perhaps twenty or thirty minutes start, they would then take up concealed positions within less than a hundred yards of the road. This was done with the idea of stimulating the powers of observation while on the move. I would then march the remainder along at the ordinary pace; the odds were with the hidden men, so the scores were made on the basis that a marching man got two points to his credit for each hidden man he discovered, while the hidden man was given one point if he was not found.

For men who were to be scouts this sort of training was of great value, as the power of seeing is of course of the utmost importance, and strange to say it is by no means an easy thing to teach, or perhaps I should say, develop. In order to accomplish the desired results it was necessary to make the work as interesting as possible. The competitive scoring was a great success and the men became extremely keen in trying to win the highest number of points. In doing so they developed really remarkable cleverness in concealing themselves at the same time being able to get a clear view of the road, without which the whole point would have been lost. At the same time the men learned how to use their eyes, so they saw many things that ordinarily would have been passed by unobserved.

To stimulate still further this power of observation I sometimes sent the men off in pairs with instructions to note anything they saw while on their way to a certain place, then accompanying the men over the same ground I would check I carefully their notes and observations. This taught them not only to see but to understand the value of the information obtained.

Another phase of the instructional work was teaching the practical use of the prismatic compass, not alone as an aid to marching in a straight line either by day or night, but as a means, in conjunction with a map, of finding one's whereabouts, or the placing definitely of some object of special interest or importance. At first the men were frightened at the idea of doing anything so complicated, but in a very short time they became quite proficient, and were able to work out their position on the map to within a few yards, simply by means of observed angles.

It may be of interest to note in passing that when it came to the time when the knowledge which these men acquired was put to actual use they acquitted themselves splendidly. They acted as guides when our Battalion went over the top in the "Somme show." It is no easy task to keep men headed absolutely straight by compass bearings when there is no tangible object in sight, especially under terrific fire such as our poor fellows were compelled to face when they headed for the German line. I regret to say that of the forty-four Brigade scouts scarcely more than a dozen escaped either wounds or death on that fateful first of July.

On the 23rd we moved back to B——e. During this period much of my time was devoted to making sketches of the German positions, as the General was anxious to have drawings made which would enable the officers and men to identify the various landmarks at a glance. At times the sketching proved somewhat exciting, as it meant having to crawl out in the open in very exposed positions in order to obtain comprehensive views of the country.

On one particular day I rode with my orderly to within a mile or so of the front line and having left the horses in the shelter of a wood, proceeded on foot across a part of the country which was being shelled intermittently. To obtain the required view I was obliged to crawl to the crest of a bare hill some distance away from the protection of any trenches, and eventually I reached the desired position. In order to make the required compass observations, I found it necessary to sit up and so render myself unpleasantly conspicuous in the landscape; whether or not the Germans detected me I cannot say for certain but I do know that within a few minutes whizbangs began to arrive with alarming regularity. Occasionally by way of variety a larger shell would come and throw a great column of earth in the air, or a shrapnel would send a shower of lead all about the neighbourhood; curiously enough all these shot fell in a semi-circle in front of me and about a hundred to a hundred and fifty yards away. Now making sketches with proper precision is a very enjoyable occupation in a peaceful place, but when one is drawing a minute piece of detail, and a noisy shell comes along screaming and scattering metal in a most indiscriminate manner, one's hand does not keep as steady as it should and I found my sketches were decorated with sundry unnecessary lines which meant nothing to the casual observer, but each scratch showed that I had been scared, so scared indeed that I wondered whether the years I had devoted to the gentle arts of drawing and painting could not have been spent to better advantage learning how to dodge enemy shells.

However, the work had to be done, and after an hour or so I became somewhat used to the conditions, and even found myself enjoying the exquisite singing of the larks. It was surprising how little attention they paid to the sound of the shells. The beauty of the uninhabited landscape in this No Man's Land made one of the many sharp contrasts of this strange scene. It had been abandoned by the farmers for nearly two years and the ground instead of bearing rich crops of grain was covered with a mass of scarlet poppies, growing in riotous profusion as far as the eye could see, a strange wild garden, its colour red as the blood that was soon to be shed so lavishly along this great battlefield of the Somme.

Cutting through the deserted fields were the narrow, white, chalk-edged trenches, our own and those of the Germans, like giant white threads, forming a net-work over the rolling country. In the middle distance red-roofed villages nestled snugly among the rich green woods, the very picture of peace, broken only by the endless communicating trench systems. These were the arteries of modern warfare through which flowed the living blood in the form of man. Still further beyond in the blue mists of the summer day were more woods, some large, some mere dots of green, and more villages almost lost in the filmy atmosphere. Here and there the burst of a large shell disturbed the beautiful scene and made one realise how deceptive was the air of tranquillity.

Sometimes it is rather difficult to locate one's exact position owing to the lack of landmarks which may be used for observation, and in order to check the panoramic drawings it is quite necessary that the point from which the observations are made shall be accurately given. While I was crouching low, at the same time trying to get my head high enough from the ground to enable me to discover well-defined landmarks, I spotted a wind-mill. Now all wind-mills are marked on our maps, so they are most useful, even when wrecked, as they usually are anywhere near the scene of activities. Having secured a careful compass reading on my wind-mill which protruded over the edge of a nearby hill, I searched vainly on my map for the said mill. True there was one more or less in the supposed direction, but taking that in connection with my other reference points placed me between the first and second line of Boche trenches, a most unhealthy position, not at all suited to my timid nature. I puzzled over the question and finally took a chance and stood upright for a minute fraction of a second.

To my great surprise the "wind-mill" proved to be the spire of the church at Albert, the Leaning Virgin appearing as one of the arms. This extraordinary metal statue of the Virgin Mary and the Child Jesus, though weighing tons, was partly dislodged by a German shell, but instead of falling it only leaned over at right-angle to the tower, and in this strange attitude it has remained ever since, though the church is completely wrecked. According to popular superstition the war will not end until the statue has fallen. According to recent reports Albert has been captured by the Germans. If this is true the bronze statue will probably be taken away and melted down for the manufacture of shells.

As a rule when out on sketching excursions I preferred to go alone, it reduced the risk of being seen. One man being less than half as conspicuous as two, and it seemed scarcely fair to ask a fellow to crawl about in exposed places and keep him there doing nothing. The inactivity is not good for any one's nerves, besides having the man with me was always an inducement to hurry the work, and so, as I said, I prefer going alone. This preference placed me in a curious predicament one day when I had to crawl out into No Man's Land in front of a piece of our trench which was very thinly occupied.

None of the men holding our line had seen me go over, for the day was so quiet that beyond a very occasional rifle shot there was no sign of activity in the sector. It was this quietness which induced me to go out in front where I could secure a particularly good view. The sketch being finished, the last part done rather hurriedly owing to the unpleasant attentions of an enemy sniper, I returned, crawling on my tummy in as inconspicuous and rapid a manner as possible to our trenches. Just as I reached the parapet, when I was by no means anxious for any delay, a broad Scotch voice hailed me and wanted to know who the - I was and what the - I was doing. (I won't give the exact words because when a Scot becomes emphatic his language does not look well in cold print.) I tried to explain who I was and what I was doing, and even showed my Brigade badge, all the time trying with considerable persistence to get on what should have been the safe side of the parapet. The shelter of the trench made a particularly strong appeal to me owing to the frequent shots which came unduly adjacent to my anatomy. But I was very much between the devil and the sea for the Scot insisted on keeping me covered with his rifle while he wanted to know where my orderly was.

In my enthusiasm for the work I had for the moment quite forgotten that an officer was not allowed to walk through the trenches unaccompanied by his orderly. So I replied that I had left my orderly to wait for me in B——e wood.

Fortunately at this moment an officer came along and he kindly allowed me to get into the trench that I might finish the argument without the assistance of bullets, and it was astonishing how great was my affection for that particular trench. However, my troubles were not yet over, as the officer hearing that I had been seen coming from the direction of the enemy's lines, - they were scarcely two hundred yards away, - decided that I must be placed under arrest, and I was duly taken before the commanding officer. I tried to explain who and what I was and why I had been out in front of the lines, but he did not seem to like my face and was very suspicious. In the end I induced him to telephone H. Q. and get a description of my facial adornments, etc. The result was that eventually I was released, much to the disappointment of the man who had first spotted me; poor fellow, he was sure that he had landed a German spy, and it was a great pity to have disappointed him.

As I made my way back, the advisability of obeying the order regarding going unaccompanied got safely into my brain, and I determined that not again would I be caught playing a lone hand. On returning to billets I passed through the woods of B——e and was interested to see what great changes had taken place since the days when we had been stationed in the neighbourhood. Wherever we looked there were guns, large guns, very large guns and small ones of every kind and description. All hidden most cunningly in every available position, the woods fairly bristled with them and the sight was good to behold. Our friend the enemy had something coming to him and the thought made me very happy.

As my orderly remarked, "The Boche is certainly going to get hell when all those guns get going."

Well, it was about time, he had been giving us a good dose of hell for a long while, and it was only fair that we should return something. The one-sided game is good enough but it becomes very monotonous after a while.

Among my various duties I had to spend some days in an F. O. P. (forward observation post) as observation officer. This meant that I must report both our own and the enemy's fire. The number and size of shells and the results of the work. An O. P. or "O. *Pip*," as it is usually called (the letter P being pronounced "pip" to avoid being mistaken for B while speaking on the telephone), is constructed with the utmost care to render it as inconspicuous as possible, while it offers a comprehensive view. The opening through which one is supposed to see everything is a long, narrow, horizontal slit, commonly called a "squint hole," which must be invisible from the front view. Smoking in the place is strictly prohibited as the smoke curling through the slit would proclaim to the enemy the position of the post, and would result in a most undesirable and immediate shelling. The greenhorn will occasionally thrust the end of a telescope at the very edge of the opening and this always results in an extraordinary and very prompt flow of language from his fellow occupants, much to the surprise of Lieut. Greenhorn, who comes to the conclusion that his fellow beings are unduly particular and perhaps rather cowardly. But he soon learns his lesson, and having learned it usually regains his popularity. Telephones are connected to the various batteries and headquarters so that all information is sent and received with promptness.

The work of the artillery F. O. O.[2] is of the utmost importance. He reports the shots of his batteries and gives instruction as to any changes necessary in range and direction and generally acts as the eye of the gunners. Accuracy is of course most desirable for the slightest mistake may cause untold trouble. There was an instance of this sort related to me that will give an idea of what momentary carelessness may accomplish. In the O. P., shown on the diagram, was the officer observing for his batteries, their direction being designated by the arrow. Several shots having been fired with the desired effect at the point in the enemy trenches marked "A" the F. O. O. wished his battery to give some attention to the point marked "B" where there was reason to believe the enemy had a trench mortar battery concealed, so he telephoned to fire at a point so many degrees left, *but forgot to increase the range*, Scarcely had he sent the message than he remembered the omission and realising that the change of direction would bring the shots directly on to the O. P., he quickly seized the telephone with the intention of rectifying the mistake before it was too late, but the wires had been cut by a shell. Of course there was no time to find the break, to get out of the post was the only thing possible. As he was in the act of giving the men instructions to make a bolt for it, the first shell from his own battery landed, a direct hit on the O. P. The unfortunate officer was instantly killed as were two

---

2. Forward observation officer.

of the men. The others though more or less injured succeeded in making their escape.

One day when I was in the O. P. a battery of large guns was trying to find a very troublesome enemy gun which was situated about a mile in front of us, and was believed to be in a certain small wood. We were told to watch the effect of the shooting at a given moment. In due course we heard the big shell humming through the air, it fell about seventy yards to the right of the little wood where it kicked up a bit of earth, but it proved to be a "dud" and like all good and well-behaved duds it failed to explode. A moment later with the aid of my glasses I saw a German leave the shelter of the trees and go to where the "dud" lay partly buried. He bent down and examined it with the evident intention of reading the markings on the nosecap in order that he might know how far it had come, and so get the range of our battery. Having found what he wanted he returned to the place where his gun was so cleverly concealed, resolving no doubt to "find" our gun later on. But he had given us the exact position of his own battery, and naturally no time was lost in communicating this interesting fact to our gunners, who sent three shells in quick succession, and it was with the greatest satisfaction that we saw a terrific explosion occur in the place where our foolish Hun had disappeared into the woods. Result: exit German battery including the foolish Hun.

On June 1st we moved to M——e. The billet assigned to me was in a small partly ruined cottage, partly ruined inasmuch as it lacked a fair share of its original roof, one wall was half gone, and another had a decent-sized hole in it, and of course there was no glass in the windows. Still it was not a bad billet considering that it was entirely exposed to the fire of the enemy whose trenches could be seen from the roof. How it happened that any of the building remained was a mystery.

My admirable servant promptly proceeded to make me comfortable, from some unknown source (I never asked awkward questions) he procured some straw for my bed, and when one sleeps on cold and highly irregular tiling whose symmetry has been disturbed by sundry chunks of iron from bursting shells, the straw is a most comforting substratum to the "flea-bag." A partly broken packing-case came (probably) from the quartermaster or the A. S. C.[3], that was my washstand, another box served as a chair, after various protruding nails had been removed, and the inevitable bottle devoted itself to holding a precious candle. My room was complete with all the luxury that any one could wish, and I only hoped the Hun would abstain from his customary careless habit of dropping shells on unoffending officers and damaging their "'appy 'omes."

It was arranged that I should mess with my old friends, the officers of company - the jolliest lot of fellows that ever lived. Our mess billet was a large house in unusually good condition on the side of the village nearest the Germans. In front of us on one side was a large open field which was unused because of its exposed position. The village itself though frequently shelled still contained a fair number of its original civilian population, and they in most cases kept shops from which we procured various luxuries - at war-zone prices, of course.

It was early in the afternoon when we arrived, very hot and very dusty. Oranges were suggested as food befitting the occasion. So one of the servants was sent out for some. He returned in a short time with a large bag of very inferior fruit purchased at a very superior price. The first orange taken from the bag was partly bad. Now a bad orange is a tempting missile and this fact was discovered by the fellow who examined it - *Biff*, and it went across the room narrowly missing a fellow's head and smashing itself in a nasty juicy mess on the wall. Needless to say within a few seconds an orange fight was in full swing, seven full-grown, able-bodied men all going it as hard as they could.

Suddenly above the sounds of laughter came the screeching of a shell, followed almost immediately by a loud explosion. But this did not in any way interfere with the orange fight. One fellow indeed stopped for a second to see where the shell had landed - it was about one hundred and fifty yards from the house - and as he looked through the broken window several oranges caught him, direct hits they were, as he had

---

3. Army Service Corps.

not had time to dodge. For nearly an hour the orange fight and the *strafing* continued and only for brief moments when a shell would come extremely near did any one stop to look at them. I relate this incident because it shows two things; first, the delightful boyish good spirits of our fellows, who can of course be quite serious enough when it is necessary; and second, how little attention is paid to ordinary shell fire as men become so thoroughly accustomed to it.

The day after our arrival at M——e, I received news from home which made my immediate return for a few days most urgent. Unfortunately my regular leave was not due for nearly two weeks, but as I was on the Brigade staff my going would not interfere with the leave of any one else, so I applied to the General, stating that I would gladly give up my full ten days, due later, if only I could have three clear days at once. To my surprise and delight my full ten days' leave was granted and needless to say after I had handed over my work, and made out the necessary reports, I lost not a second in packing and getting off.

Bairnsfather - bless him for the good laughs that he has given us - has depicted in his delightful drawings some of the incidents connected with the "leave train." I feel that it is scarcely necessary for me to do more than suggest that the reader glance at those drawings and he will understand the situation of the man who goes on leave. Trains *may* go slower, and stop *more* frequently, and be *more* crowded, but I doubt it. Of course every one is impatient to get home once he starts, even though the actual time of leave does not begin till you are on the boat.

To make matters worse when we got to Amiens we had the mortification of reading the *first* report of the naval battle of Jutland and nothing more depressing was ever offered for the consumption of a Britisher. It is difficult to depress men going on leave from the front, but seldom have I seen a more sober lot than we were.

To be beaten on land was one thing; of course we quite expected to get an occasional smash, but on the sea, it was unthinkable. Yet there it was in cold black and white. We read it and re-read it and some fellow finally remarked, "Oh, I bet there's something wrong," and thank Heaven he was right.

Eventually, notwithstanding the sundry and various delays, we reached England. How delightfully peaceful it seemed! No appearance of war, every one cheerful, yes, it certainly was nice to be home, even if the object of my coming was a dreary one, for the war had hit me hard, so hard indeed that I had been forced to sell my house; it was a wrench, but after all there was no use in worrying, the thing had to be done.

Every one in England was talking about the impending offensive, the air was full of expectancy and hope. The coming show was to finish the war according to the general idea and we were all to be home for Christmas. The munition workers had given up their holidays that they might be able to furnish shells to the very limit of their power, and the Hun was to discover England's might. This was all very fine and I hoped the popular predictions would be correct. Of course I was not allowed to tell anything about what was going on at the front, nor when the offensive was to start.

By way of information I may tell the reader in strict confidence that of course I did not know, though when I said so in reply to the oft-repeated question, it would be received with a knowing wink. People do not realise how very little information is given to us at the front. Most of our news comes from the English papers which frequently we receive on the day of publication. Then we have "Comic Cuts" as the official account of the daily happenings connected with the world's war is disrespectfully called; beyond these sources of information we know very little.

My short leave ended only too soon, and once more I found myself on the platform with hundreds of others headed for the "trenches" and the platform was as usual crowded with those heroic women who tried to look cheerful in spite of the fact that in their hearts they knew what was to come within a few weeks, and no matter whether the big offensive was a success or not, the toll would be enormous. Yet tears were withheld and smiles prevailed. What those smiles cost, God alone knows.

The return to France was made with the rapidity which characterises all journeys which lead away from home. Delays would have been almost welcome, but they did not happen. Connections were made with aggravating punctuality, in marked contrast to the apparent slowness and delays of the homeward-bound trains.

At Amiens the train was supposed to wait about half an hour, so I took the opportunity to see the R. T. O. (the Railroad Transport Officer; he is the general information bureau who is supposed to know where every unit is, or should be, and how you are to find your way to it). There were many ahead of me and when I finally reached the good chap and asked him where our Brigade might be found, he told me with quiet unconcern that my train, the one on which I had come, was due to have started five minutes ago. I rushed out and along the platform just in time to see it disappearing in the smoky distance, on it was all my kit. Had I been homeward bound this would have been a calamity, but under the conditions I took it most philosophically and simply contented myself with wiring ahead to my station requesting the M. P. (Military Police - very useful people!) to take the kit out of the train. A good meal being quite in order, the time between then and the departure of the next train, and fortunately there was a next one, was spent to the best advantage.

In due course I reached my destination which by good fortune was La N——e and reported to the Brigade Major. Then I was told that our Brigadier had left us. This was a great blow for we were all very fond of him. He was badly broken up at the sudden change as he had looked forward with the keenest interest to the coming offensive in the preparation for which he had worked so hard. The following day his successor arrived. He was a much younger man and he immediately won our hearts by his kindness and good humour and very business-like ways. This was his first Brigade and naturally he was much pleased with life. It has never been my good fortune to be among a finer lot than those on the staff. The Brigade Major in particular was, I think, the most delightful man I have ever known and as my work was almost entirely with him, I felt more than content.

We spent much of our time making notes and sketches of positions, and in visiting the trenches that the Brigade was to occupy in the "Push," and I had to take the scouts to a point overlooking the front and explain the various landmarks and what would be the scouts' part in the coming attack. For it was now no longer a secret that the big offensive was to begin within a couple of weeks, and of course every one was keyed up with excitement. The men did not mind how hard the work was, they never do when the object is clear. The scouts were intensely interested in studying the ground over which the attack was to be made, and with the aid of the panoramic sketches, in conjunction with the excellent maps with which we were furnished, they easily identified the most important features of the land. Hitherto they had only seen the country in front of our line from the trenches which are seldom constructed with the idea of affording extended views, but the point I had selected for instructional purposes was a new communication trench on a fairly high hill about four thousand feet from where we were to start in the attack. This commanded a splendid view of the enemy country and showed nearly all the trenches that were of direct interest to us.

In speaking of the maps we use it might be of interest to the reader to know with what extreme care they are made. The reproduction opposite will give a slight idea of these maps, though owing to the reduction in its size it does not do justice to the original. All the trenches, railways, and other works carried on by the enemy are put in from aeroplane photographs. It was part of my duty each day to go over great numbers of these prints and check up the various lines. By this method every piece of new work accomplished anywhere in the enemy lines was added to the map with full detail; and as new maps could not be printed for distribution every day, I made small sketches, showing all changes and additions, and these were immediately mimeographed and sent out to all who had maps (a record is kept of the distribution of all maps). By this means they could record the alterations and keep the maps corrected to date. Occasionally, when the additions had been of sufficient importance, the maps were reprinted and given to all who were interested in the particular part of the line.

Chapter IX
Hell Let Loose

ON JUNE THE 20th we left La N——e and the kind people turned out to wish us *"Bon chance."* They knew we were to he in the fight very soon, and that in ail probability the Battalion would not again return to the village that had been its favourite billet. Our next stop was at V——e, which we found crowded to its extreme limit with men, and consequently very uncomfortable. The poor Town Major was at his wits' end to find accommodation for us. Every village in the area was in the same condition owing to the necessity of concentrating the vast number of troops needed for the "Show."

On the morning of the 24th the great preliminary bombardment commenced. The greatest concentration of gun fire ever indulged in by the British up to that time. At last the Boche was to learn our strength and the learning must have been a decidedly painful experience. Everywhere, for miles back of our front line, guns of all sizes were belching death- dealing missiles with tireless energy. Ammunition was practically unlimited, and it was our intention to destroy completely every part of the German trenches, cut all their masses of barbed wire, and level every building in the village strongholds. Nothing was to be left standing or intact. Complete annihilation and only that would satisfy us.

But we did not know how deep were the German dugouts, nor did we fully understand their plan of defence, which included the safeguarding in these dugouts of innumerable machine guns, the instrument most dreaded by the infantry. From these by many ingenious devices the guns would be quickly brought up to the surface of the ground as soon as our guns raised their fire, in order that the infantry might go forward. We were soon to learn a great and important lesson, but at the cost of much good blood.

In the meantime our guns continued the good work to the intense satisfaction of Thomas Atkins & Co. Whenever the men had an hour to spare they would make for the nearest vantage point and watch the endless explosions as our shells landed along the enemy lines and threw up columns of smoke and earth to unbelievable heights.

Overhead our aeroplanes darted about like huge dragon-flies, patrolling the sky and keeping the enemy planes so far back of their own lines that for them no observing of our guns was possible. In this particular region we had absolute supremacy in the air.

Toward evening of this first day every officer and man not actually on duty was watching the "Show." By daylight it was wonderful, the bursting shells causing many shaped and many coloured columns to cut into the sky-line, but at night it was a far more impressive sight. The whole country before us as far as the eye could see was apparently on fire, dark clouds hanging low in the sky reflected the deep red and orange of the endless shells, while the cold blue-white Verey lights trailed in graceful curves through the violated sky. Here and there signals of green and red rockets gave variety to the scene and caused satisfaction to our fellows, for it showed that Mr. Hun was in trouble.

Once in a while there would be a terrific explosion which dwarfed the noise and glare of all the bursting shells and we knew that an ammunition dump had been hit and again there would be satisfaction among our men for it meant there would be that much less ammunition for the Hun to give us.

Occasionally the firing would partly, or entirely subside, and perhaps for half an hour or so scarcely a shot would be fired. Then suddenly hell would be let loose, for every gun as though actuated by one invisible hand, would spit forth its deadly shot, and the air would vibrate with the roar as of ten thousand peals of thunder, again would the enemy lines be lighted up with the golden glow of battle, and again would Thomas Atkins smile and make jests, which, though not always conspicuous for their refinement, were invariably funny.

This ubiquitous humour is wonderful. No matter what happens, especially if it is something which causes him or his comrades great personal discomfort, he always manages to find an amusing remark. While a really good explosion in the enemy country calls for an avalanche of wit which to be thoroughly appreciated must be heard under the proper conditions.

The bombardment continued day and night with more or less regularity. The spells of quiet were almost invariably followed by "intense" periods and we could not help wondering how the poor devils in front of us were getting along. So far as could be seen from our various high places, the front line trenches to the left of Fricourt (the part in which we were so vitally interested) were completely demolished. Instead of the even line of chalk parapets we could distinguish endless craters touching each other in a way which spoke well for the work of our gunners. Of the trenches further back little or nothing was discernible, but from the numerous bursts of shell it was evident that proper attention was being given to everything within range.

On the 26th we were told that a big gas attack was to be launched. Our men had with great labour carried the unwieldy cylinders up to the front line a few nights ago, and naturally enough they were as anxious as we were to see the attack. The weather was perfect, a slight and favourable wind and no immediate sign of rain. Shortly before the appointed hour there was a furious bombardment lasting several minutes. This was intended to make the Germans keep out of sight so that they would not see the gas, then immediately before this ended the gas was liberated along various parts of our line. The poisonous yellowish smoke drifted across No Man's Land in the most approved way, and we all felt a fiendish delight in watching it.

The dastardly attack on the wretched Canadians and others at Ypres was still fresh in our minds, and now the nation which, in violation of all international law and against all traditions of decency in warfare, had started this most damnable form of fighting ever dreamed of was to be hoist with its own petard. Its own soldiers,; poor creatures, were to suffer as the Canadians and some of our home troops had suffered. They were to die in agonies as those Canadians had died - agonies such as no man has ever known, and we were glad that the British, who above all things like to fight in a clean, sportsman-like way, had taken off the gloves and were fighting the devil with his own weapons.

We prayed that the time might come when the brutal Hun would curse the day that he had polluted the earth with this vile gas, this breath of hell, the taint of which will rise whenever the ruthless war party of Germany is spoken of. It was as though two boxers were in the ring and one, finding that he could not win fairly, threw vitriol into the face of his opponent and then downed him when he was blinded and helpless. The pick of the German soldiers could not conquer those heroes at Ypres by fair means even though they were vastly superior in numbers and in artillery equipment, and so, in cowardly determination to win at any cost, they used the gas which had been made several years before and kept ready for just such an emergency. But God was with us and the heroic resistance offered by our suffering men must stand forever as a monument to them, while a monument of quite a different kind will stand for the fiendish brutality of Germany.

Such were the thoughts which ran through our minds as in silence we watched those slowly moving death-dealing clouds that poisoned the very ground they crossed. Had any one told us two years before that we, who called ourselves civilised people, would have stood still and actually taken satisfaction in watching our men fight with such means we would have refused to believe it.

Do not think, kind reader (if you are one who has not been in the fight), that this means that we are becoming brutalised, not at all. No man is more human or humane than our fellows at the front. The stories of their unselfish kindness and sympathy would fill volumes, but this is a war for our existence, and for the existence of all we hold most dear, freedom in its greatest sense, with the right for all to live decently, whether they be strong or weak, and against those who threaten our right we must fight with whatever weapons they choose. We accepted their choice of weapons when the duel started. It was to be guns, and they had the greater ones, and their numbers were incalculably greater. Yet we accepted. Then they decided to fight with gas, yes, and liquid fire, and every horror known to science, and we too have called in our scientists, and we too will use gas and every other form of horror. This has been asked for by Germany and she shall have all she gives and the measure shall be filled and pressed down, and it shall overflow. We shall compete with the Germans in all things save one, the committing of atrocities, in that she may reign supreme, but in everything else she must take second place.

The gas attack we were watching on this beautiful day of June lasted less than half an hour, so far as we could see, but for those unfortunate creatures in the enemy trenches the effects were of much longer duration. They probably thought that we intended to launch our attack as soon as the gas got in its deadly work and to ward it off they put up a terrific barrage or curtain of fire across our front line, thereby wasting a lot of ammunition, but it gave them the satisfaction of imagining that they had succeeded in preventing our attack.

Owing to the arrival of vast numbers of cavalry the Brigade staff together with one Battalion, machine gunners and sundry other parts of our unit were instructed to move from V——e to B——e. At one o'clock we were to leave so the men were given dinner before starting. In Brigade H. Q. we were about half-way through our lunch when the familiar *whooooooo* of a shell interrupted the conversation. The beastly thing seemed to be coming directly for us, and we expected to see it land on the table. Suddenly there was a terrific explosion, the shell had dropped in the centre of a courtyard about one hundred and fifty yards in front of us. Unfortunately a number of our men were in this yard having their meal. The scene which resulted was indescribable, and in the midst of it all, the cries of the mutilated and dying men were drowned by the roars of another and still another shell. The second shot accounted for a number of our men in the street when they had assembled to move to B——e. The third one landed in a garden one hundred yards from our H. Q. where it killed a poor little girl who was playing with her kitten.

Relief for the many wounded was needed immediately, but the doctors and all their staff had left for B——e, so there was a delay, as unfortunate as it was unavoidable. How small a thing influences lives, only by the merest chance had it been decided that we should not leave V——e until after lunch. According to the original plan we were to have gone at eleven that morning. Had we done so this ghastly misfortune would not have happened.

That evening in the new quarters our Brigade following the usual custom in the British Army indulged in an open-air day-before-the-battle concert which was thoroughly well attended. Except for a few seats arranged for the officers it was a case of "standing room only," not alone was every inch of standing room in the square courtyard taken, but the surrounding buildings were occupied inside and out, that is to say windows and roofs. A small rough stage had been erected on which a piano was placed. This instrument had very evidently not been tuned since the war began, or perhaps since the war of 1870. Anyhow it was *not* in tune. However, that made little difference. Among the four Battalions there was quite a fair share of talent. Some of it was professional, but the greater part was amateur, or very much amateur.

The poets of the Brigade had been very busy, especially the wags, and as this was an extra special night there was considerable license allowed, with the result that any of our officers who were possessed of peculiarities had them thoroughly aired to the great amusement of all hands. No one was respected from the Brigadier down. Some of the songs were decidedly amusing, at times even witty. Of course there was a sprinkling of the mawkish sentimental stuff that so thoroughly delights some of our people; the "Don't kick your mother when she's down," and "The pore girl hadn't got no friends" type. There were topical songs on the Kaiser and his kind, in fact no subject was neglected and all were sung to the accompaniment of the guns which never for a moment ceased. But though we all laughed a great deal, to many of us there was something unspeakably sad about the whole performance. It was almost as though a number of men, condemned to death, were giving a minstrel show on the eve of their execution.

A great many of those fine jovial fellows who were singing funny songs or laughing so vociferously to-night would be laying stark and still within a very few hours, and as each one would mount the rude platform and do his part in the entertainment I found myself wondering whether he was one of those doomed to make the great sacrifice. Yet in spite of the conditions it was a jolly evening and one could not help admiring the splendid spirits and remarkable behaviour of the men, for though this was the last night on which any liquor, beer, or wine would be bought or used, there was not a man present who was the worse for drink. The morrow held no terror for them. The Great Push was to be the greatest adventure of their lives, and their one thought was that at last the time was come when we were to know whether our civilians' army had been sufficiently trained to stand successfully against Germany's professional army, and judging from the attitude of our men they felt not the slightest doubt as to the outcome.

Scarcely had the concert (so called for lack of a better name) ended than to our disgust a gentle rain commenced. If there was one thing: we needed more than another to make our offensive a success it was fine weather. Rain, apart from the frightful personal discomfort, meant a marked decrease in the efficiency of our shells, and added enormous difficulties to the advance of the infantry and artillery. The ground was composed largely of chalk, which when wet became so slippery that in the open, and still more so in the trenches, a man heavily laden with all the paraphernalia of battle could make headway only with the greatest difficulty. So we dreaded rain, but our dreading it seemed to make no difference, for it continued all that night and most of the following day. The attack was to have been made early in the morning of the 29th and already part of our Brigade had gone to their positions in the line when the order came that the "Show" was postponed for forty-eight hours. Any one would have thought from the attitude of the men, when this bad news was broken to them, that they had been told their leave was cancelled, which is the worst news a man can get at the front. Never have I seen men, so depressed and disappointed. Nothing could console them, not even such remarks as one in broad Yorkshire which I happened to overhear.

"Don't th' care, Tom, thou's got coople more days to live." The delay though unavoidable was most unfortunate for it undoubtedly knocked out a lot of the enthusiasm which is such a valuable asset in an attack. However it could not be helped and we spent the two days doing nothing as assiduously as possible, but in spite of all our efforts the hours dragged along with painful slowness.

Chapter X
Battle of the Somme – The Great Day

THE DAY HAD at last arrived when we were to move forward, yes, really forward, when we were to know whether the months of preparation and training were to give the great results that we all hoped for, and many expected. What terrific activity had been concentrated daring these months, not alone in the field armies but at home and abroad where the gigantic supplies of ammunition had been made. From the mines which produced the metals, and the ships which had brought the supplies to England, the feverish activity in the great factories which had been turning out guns of all sorts and sizes, and all types of shells, from those required for the little field gun to the monster implements of destruction weighing more than a ton apiece, to the endless supplies of all kinds needed in such vast quantities.

Then the bringing of all this material to France. What a story that in itself would make. How the vessels were brought through the submarine and mine-infested seas and what careful management had been necessary. It had indeed been a period of elaborate and colossal preparation such as the world has never known, and now we were to make use of all this great thought and labour. We were to launch our first really big attack against the so-called impregnable position of the Germans. We were to know within a few hours whether or not our new armies would prove equal to the task of beating the highly trained soldiers of Germany. That we should succeed no one of us for a moment ever doubted. We were full of that splendid hope and trust which coupled with the wonderful cheerful spirits of the British soldier, be he of the old thoroughly trained lot or of the new army, which makes up in enthusiasm what it may lack in training, carries through to ultimate victory regardless of the difficulties encountered.

It was on the 30th day of June that we moved, each Battalion leaving its billets at the appointed minute while the men bid good-bye to the little village of B——e, the little village where we had spent so many jolly days, and which was never again to be seen by a large proportion of those cheerful fellows who sang and cheered as they passed along the white dusty street. The songs they sang as they marched to battle were not of deeds of valour, nor were they of battle at all, far from it - just cheerful ones expressing deep sentiment and feeling. As the splendid fellows vanished into distance I heard:

"Keep the home fires burning while your hearts are yearning
Though your lads are far away they dream of home.
There's a silver lining through the dark cloud shining;
Turn the dark clouds inside out till the boys come home."

It was sung as a message of comfort and hope and was the very spirit of the men, showing how they are always thinking of home, of those who are waiting and watching and dreading the news which the next few hours might bring.

It was my duty to remain with the Brigade Staff which would of course be the last to leave. I therefore had the opportunity to watch the four Battalions move away, and bid farewell, and Godspeed, to as good a lot of fellows as ever lived. Fortunately one does not have much time for thinking under such conditions for there is endless work to be done, and every moment is precious so the day passed only too quickly.

Toward evening, having left our possessions in the care of those who must remain behind we (the Brigadier, the Staff Major, the Brigade bombing and signalling officers and myself) rode forward to within a mile of the front line. Then we dismounted, sent the horses back, and continued on foot through the crowded communication trenches toward the Brigade dugout. The noise of the incessant bombardment was simply appalling. It seemed as though every gun in the whole country was firing at maximum speed, and the late evening sky was a great glow of crimson and orange, as the shells burst along the enemy lines. The scene was grandly impressive for it showed with what power the great offensive was being undertaken. The long dreary months of inactivity had ended. The dearth of guns and shells, which for nearly two years had been a continued source of chagrin and mortification to us, was now a thing of the past. Apparently our supplies of all the material necessary for the conduct of a great modern war were unlimited, and it put heart into us to a degree that can scarcely be comprehended by those who have had no part in the actual fighting.

As we passed groups of moving or resting men it was a pleasure to watch their faces. A glorious cheerfulness was reflected in every countenance. That the great chance of death within a very few hours was certain did not manifest itself in any way, and well might the casual observer have thought from the endless jokes and laughter that these splendid men were a lot of boys on their way to a game, rather than that they were going into what was destined to be one of the biggest battles the world had ever known. It made one proud to belong to a race which can take the most serious side of life with such magnificent spirit, a spirit which nothing can crush, and which temporary defeat makes only more evident and irresistible.

The long walk through that narrow crowded trench was very tedious, but eventually we reached the Brigade Headquarters dugout, which was within a stone's throw of the actual front-line trench, and there found the staff of messengers and signallers, telephonists, etc., already at their places. The dugout, like all of ours, was a roughly-made temporary affair, so very different from the elaborate structures made by the Germans, and it seemed to reflect the difference in the point of view of the two sides. We regarded our stay on the Somme line as of transient interest, as we intended to move forward as soon as possible, while the Germans apparently built their complicated and wonderful underground lines for an indefinite period of occupation, in fact as though they expected to remain in them for the rest of their natural lives, as indeed many of them did.

Needless to say every inch of trench space was occupied, not only with men, but with supplies of all kinds, such as ammunition, bombs, stretchers, picks, shovels, wire, water, and the hundred and one things that might be needed when we moved forward. Over the trenches were numerous artillery bridges to allow the guns to be rushed forward without a moment's delay after the infantry had reached the German lines, scaling ladders lined every trench to assist the men in doing the "parapet hop" with the least possible difficulty. Everything that careful thought and foresight could provide for had been done. As each unit arrived it took up its position according to the prearranged plans. There was seething activity, but no confusion, except possibly when an enemy shell landed in a crowded area and sent a group of wretched men to eternity.

In the Brigade dugout the telephones were constantly busy reporting all that was going on. Each company on arrival would, of course, report to the Brigadier and by 2 A.M. every man was accounted for, and we had to wait patiently for the passing of the few hours that remained before the zero minute would arrive. All watches were carefully synchronised but so far as we were concerned the zero remained a mystery, kept absolutely secret by those in command.

Dawn came slowly over that rumbling area. A cool clear dawn, lighted by a sun which fought its way through the heavy smoke-laden atmosphere. Between the angry reports of exploding shells, and the crackling of the machine guns, came the liquid notes of the larks, singing in the sky, as unconcerned as though they had always lived in the midst of hurtling shells. In the woods back of Fricourt the voice of the cuckoo could be heard, and it seemed strangely out of place. One always associates it with the quiet of the country and here it was mingling its sweet notes with the ghastly droon of the passing shells, and the terrific explosions which shook the very earth.

Above all, our aeroplanes policed the sky watching the enemy's lines with hawk-like keenness. Throughout the trenches there was a strange ominous quiet. A suppressed excitement pervaded everywhere. Men spoke in hushed voices. The great moment must soon come when they were to prove themselves men. As they talked they smoked incessantly. At no time is the cigarette more blessed than during the period preceding an attack, when the minutes move so slowly, and the pulse beats with undue speed.

Higher and higher rose the sun that memorable first day of July, 1916. Its warmth was grateful to the huddled masses of waiting men, for under keen but suppressed excitement one feels a queer coldness that is almost painful - the throat becomes parched and the tongue dry and hard. Word was finally passed along that 7.30 was to be the zero minute, and with this knowledge there was a sense of relief, for then all knew that the suspense would soon end. Hot tea was served to the men as they ate their breakfasts and what a Godsend that tea was. Surely no army was ever taken care of in the matter of food as ours has been in France. Seldom if ever is there any hitch in the arrangements and food comes with a regularity, and of a quality, that is a constant source of surprise and wonder, notwithstanding the existing conditions which so often are more than unfavourable.

Seven-fifteen came at last and with it a terrific intense bombardment of the enemy's lines. The whole horizon was a great cloud of bursting shells. More and more shells tore through the air, and rained death and destruction on the wretched Germans, and we could not but feel a sense of pity for the poor creatures who had to undergo such a devastating fire. It must have been hellish, and they had been having this with only slight intermission for eight long days.

Just before the minute hand pointed to the half hour the bombardment eased up, and only the barrage fire over the second and third lines was continued. Then at the exact moment our whole line from Thièpval to near Fay (the French having the part on our right southward from Bray) emerged from the trenches, and No Man's Land over which for nearly two years no human being had dared to venture, except under the deceptive darkness of night, was covered with wave after wave of thin lines of khaki-clad men marching slowly and steadily toward the German trenches.

Heavens! what a picture that was. What a grand picture of courage and discipline!

As far as one could see, on either side, those lines moved with a deadly precision, facing a withering machine gun fire which thinned their ranks at an appalling rate, until of the first lines but few remained, but those, God bless them, went on and on. No hesitation, no faltering, just a grim determination to go forward until stopped by bullet or shell, for nothing else could halt them. On they went over that field of vivid scarlet poppies, whose colour seemed to stand as a symbol of the fine red blood that was being shed so lavishly for the salvation of the world, while the sky-blue cornflowers, and the gleaming white of the chalk-lined trenches, together with the red poppies, gave the red, white and blue, the national colours of the British and French who were fighting side by side for the greatest cause the world has ever known (and joined now by the Americans whose colours, by happy augury, are the same).

There was so much to be done that it was impossible to give more than an occasional glance at what was going on, but apparently, barring only the terrific machine gun fire which played such havoc with our men everything was going on as planned.

Our Brigade was on the left of Fricourt, and the two Battalions of my regiment, the King's Own Yorkshire Light Infantry, were side by side on the front line of the assault while the Durhams and East Yorkshires followed in support. We were unfortunately unable to reach our more advanced objectives owing to the heavy fire, and to our great number of casualties, but we got as far as the sunken road within an hour or so. This point is on the immediate left of Fricourt, which we eventually expected to surround. The defensive works of the village were so powerful that it was not considered wise to take it by assault, but to force its evacuation by threatening to cut off the garrison. Along most of the total line of attack, about twenty miles all told, things were going well. At La Boisselle the enemy offered a very stiff resistance and at one place the assaulting troops had gone rather too far, and had omitted to clear the first and second line trenches; this unfortunately resulted in very troublesome conditions a little later that day. At Thièpval our line was unable to advance against the steep hill side and very powerfully fortified positions, but elsewhere we were succeeding splendidly as was shown by the reports which were continually coming in by telephone and runners.

At about nine o'clock our Brigadier decided to go forward with the Brigade Major to see personally how we were doing, as we had lost so heavily in officers that it was hard to get reliable information through the many field telephones which had been carried forward and whose wires were constantly cut. I was sent with certain instructions to the Headquarters' Staff and told to rejoin the Brigadier as soon as possible. He, however, had vanished when I returned some ten minutes later, and though I hunted through every trench and inquired from the men who were moving forward, and the wounded who were returning, I could get no trace of him, and so, after half an hour, I returned to the dugout, for it had suddenly occurred to me that by some oversight no officer had been left in charge and important messages might be coming in at any moment. On my way back I had to leave the trench as it was entirely blocked with wounded men who were trying to make their way back to the dressing station. It was remarkable how cheerful they were, smiling and joking about their wounds, in the most extraordinary way, and nearly all of them were smoking.

The men I passed were of many different regiments, a ghastly, bleeding, battle-marked lot. Some of my own fellows would recognise me and would laughingly ask what I thought of the regiment, how it had behaved, all so glad to have actually started the Germans on their backward path. Some would give the sad news of so-and-so's death, how he had died "grandly," as they expressed it. We had had a little reverse at Loos the previous year, which, through no fault of the men or officers, had given the whole division a slight bad mark. The men had always deeply felt and resented this and one chap who passed me managed to smile, in spite of several ghastly wounds, as he said, "Well, sir, I guess they won't hold Loos up against us now, will they?" It was rather pathetic, that he with all that suffering should have so keenly at heart the honour of the regiment, and it shows what a wonderful thing is the regimental *esprit de corps*. It leads men on to doing not only their best, but even more than their best.

In watching that gory procession it struck me what a terrible price is paid for the success of all military enterprises. Here was this line of men, who little more than an hour ago were normal men in the finest of health and strength, and now maimed, and with every degree of injury, they painfully made their way back to the human repair department. The well men were rapidly moving eastward in countless numbers, going forward to the assistance of their comrades, while the injured so labouriously dragged their way back, two human streams, the sound and the unsound. Before us, all energies were devoted to destruction; behind us, all human power and skill tried to repair the damage.

It was a severe test on the nerves of the younger and less experienced men who were going forward, for was not this returning stream a terrible object lesson of what lay before them, and each much have wondered, perhaps subconsciously, whether or not he would have the good luck to be able to form a link in the endless human chain of walking cases, or whether he would be disabled and doomed to remain out on the ground to await the kind help of the stretcher bearer; perhaps fortune would be still less kind and he might become one of those pathetic khaki figures that would never again move.

Yet there was no evidence that any one suffered in spirits by the scenes. Jokes passed between the wounded and the well, and the phrase was constantly heard, "Oh, you lucky beggar, you've got a cushy Blighty" (i.e., a "soft" wound which will take you to Blighty, the Indian word meaning England or home) or "Cheero, lad, y're going back home, give 'em my love when you get there."

Here and there a poor chap would fall exhausted, and his fellow-sufferers would try to help him along, or place him gently in a convenient recess of the trench to await the arrival of the stretcher bearers who were already over-burdened with work. No one seemed in the least downhearted, for were we not winning, were we not already safely in the German trenches, the trenches we had been staring at by day and by night for so many months, the trenches from which the well-equipped enemy had been dealing out a regular death rate to our fellows, who through lack of munitions had been unable to retaliate. And now all was changed, we were to become the upper dogs, and the Germans were to feel our fangs biting deeply, and still more deeply, until their life's blood would be let, and they would cry for the mercy which they had denied to others.

About this time the sight of the first batch of prisoners gave a great sense of satisfaction. Some thirty or forty of the grey figures came streaming across No Man's Land with hands held high, and all equipment removed. Some wore the uncouth steel helmets, some caps, while many were bareheaded, and most of them were in a pitiful state of nervousness. The effect of the long artillery bombardment was only too evident, not only causing shock to their system, but numbers had been without food and water for many hours, the heavy shelling had made it impossible to bring up rations to the more isolated positions. Altogether I felt sorry for the wretched fellows. So did our men who gave freely of their slender supplies of cigarettes and water to those who, but an hour or two earlier, they had been trying to kill. That is one of the splendid things about Tommy Atkins. He bears not the slightest resentment against his erstwhile foe. The moment he surrenders he is treated with the utmost kindness, and never once have I heard any disparaging or unkind remarks made, as long as the prisoners behave properly. This first lot seemed to be greatly relieved at being taken. For them the war was over, and their main idea was to reach as rapidly as possible a place where they would be safe from shells.

My mind was painfully busy as I made my way over the shell-torn and body strewn ground between the trenches. Machine gun bullets whistled past in ceaseless numbers and now and then a screaming shell would come and throw great masses of earth, sand bags, or even men into the air. Yet it all seemed so impersonal, so unreal, that one would not take any particular notice of it, it was as though it was meant for some other fellow. Now and then a momentary feeling of terrible, appalling fear would strike one as some ghastly incident occurred in the immediate vicinity, but the feeling would pass as quickly as it had come, and a keen interest in the great scene would take its place. I remember feeling the greatest possible desire to sit down and make sketches of the drama which was being enacted but of course there was no time, every minute being precious, and I hurried on to the dugout.

On arriving there I found calls for help. Reinforcements were urgently needed at this or that point, and these calls I passed on to the divisional headquarters. What a strange scene was that in the murky dugout. By the flickering yellow flames of a few candles, the tense faces of the telephone and telegraph operators could be seen as they took the endless messages and I could not help thinking of an exchange in any of the big cities where the hum of messages never stopped, but there the activities were all so peaceful, and so comparatively unimportant, while here the lives of men, thousands of men, hung on a single message getting through correctly, when the results of great plans trembled in the balance of a few throbs of the wire.

As an accompaniment to the unseen calls was the steady booming of the guns, great and small, our guns and those of the enemy, it all seemed like a gigantic thunderstorm of endless duration. Now and then a sweating messenger would crawl in exhausted, bringing word from some outlying company whose wires had all been broken. Perhaps the man was one of three or four who had started with duplicate messages, and where were the others? God knows, for these trusty runners who bring word across the open shell-torn area pay a heavy price for their splendid work. Yet they do not hesitate, for on them depends the welfare of many of their comrades.

Shortly before noon the Brigadier returned, and I immediately placed before him copies of all messages received and sent. Before going through them he told me that poor B——, the Brigade Major, had been killed, or at least very badly wounded by a machine gun.

They had, it appeared, gone forward of our most advanced line, in order to ascertain what was holding up our advance, when suddenly they saw the Germans rushing up to a corner of Shelter Wood where they got the gun into action with such unfortunate results. It was a terrible blow, for B—— was one of the finest men I have ever had the good fortune to meet, and I felt as though my very best friend had been killed. There was no chance of rescuing him even if he were still alive and there seemed little hope of that. Still I determined to bring back the body if a possible opportunity occurred.

Chapter XI
A Bad Night Among the Shells

During the afternoon there were endless things requiring attention. Among others was the moving of our headquarters to a wretched little dugout in a badly battered part of the trenches. Occasionally during the remaining hours of daylight I had to visit various parts of what that morning had been our front line. The sights that met one's eyes were not pretty and need not be told in detail. The terrible havoc wrought by some of the enemy shells where the men had assembled preparatory to going over the top, when whole groups of men had been annihilated beyond identification, was ghastly beyond description.

Here and there I came upon the bodies of fellows of my own lot and it made me sick to see what the poor old Battalion had suffered.

Still there was a gratification in looking over the great events of the day. The German line, which had been selected with such care, and fortified by every means known to modern military science, so that it was deemed impregnable, had fallen. In less than an hour from the moment when our men began the move, we had occupied almost the entire front lines to a depth of from one to half a dozen lines of trenches, over a front of about eighteen miles. The impossible had been accomplished. The indomitable German troops had been beaten by our new armies, and the achievement we believed marked the beginning of Germany's end as a great military power. Never again were we to yield ground to our insolent self-satisfied enemy. Slowly but steadily would we push forward. Looking back at it now, it is a great satisfaction to realise that not a gun have we lost since we began that forward move on July 1st, 1916, and the day will stand for all time as marking the vindication of

British and French armies against the foolish and undeserved slurs cast on them by the Huns, whose overbearing conceit has been doomed to such complete downfall...[4] They could not win when they fought us with overwhelming superiority of numbers and unlimited supplies of guns and ammunition, how then could they hope to win when we became more evenly matched! We had not forgotten the days when the famous thin khaki line, without reserves or big guns, stood between Calais and the German hordes. In overwhelming numbers, backed by massed artillery, these highly trained forces of the Kaiser attempted, again and again, to break through that line of immortals, and they had failed. Never again would they have such an opportunity.

Shortly after dark the Brigadier told Capt. Y—— and me to go over into the newly acquired line and gather and sort out any odd batches of men, stragglers who had become detached from their units. Also to get any useful information that we could pick up. Just before we started, three officers were handed over to our care, with instructions that they were to be delivered to certain units. Their names we did not know, and in the dark we could not see their faces. They were indeed strangers to us. We told them to follow and do exactly as we did, and under no conditions become separated. Making our way across what had been No Man's Land was a somewhat unpleasant task as the enemy kept up a constant fire, both of machine gun and artillery, so our progress was necessarily slow.

On our way we came upon one particularly badly wounded man lying in the open and he begged to be put in a nearby trench where he would be comparatively safe. I was anxious to oblige the poor chap but Capt. Y——, who was senior to me, declared that it was not our job and that we must move forward. Reluctantly I left the fellow and we continued on our precarious way, eventually arriving at the battered remains of what had been the German front line trench until that morning. Here we discovered that one of our three charges had vanished and of course we concluded he had been shot.

---

4. This was written in August, 1917.

Curiously enough seven months later when I rejoined the reserve battalion of my regiment in the North of England I found that my roommate was that very officer. He described to me how upset he had been at the incident of the wounded man being left, and how it had made him realise the stern demands of war more than any other episode in his short experience. Then he told how he had crouched in a shell hole during one of the many *strafes* and had been unable to find us when he emerged. After wandering about in a hopeless way he had become mixed up among some barbed wire and been shot through the lung. It was a curious coincidence that we should have come together after those many months, neither having known the other's name.

That night of wandering among the shell-torn German trenches, where all semblance to the original line had been obliterated, will always live in my mind as the most ghastly night of my life. The night was inky dark, the darkness made all the more overpowering by the constant flashes of exploding shells and the cold gleam of the somewhat distant Verey lights. The ground was but a mass of jagged craters into which we repeatedly fell, often landing in the midst of torn and dismembered human bodies.

Here and there we would find crouching figures, seemingly asleep. They were silent when we addressed them, and when we emphasised our remarks by a push they rolled over stiff and cold, for they were dead. Sometimes groups of living men would be found, and these were sorted out according to their units, but frequently a shell would come and their numbers would be sadly thinned. The whole thing was ghastly beyond all description and we were both glad when finally we had completed our work and turned our faces toward headquarters. To find the way in the darkness was no easy matter for we had been wandering through the labyrinth of shell craters for several hours and were compelled to trust to our sense of direction as much as to our compasses. However, at half-past one we succeeded in reaching our destination much to our own and the General's relief, for he had begun to fear we had been knocked out.

During the night written reports had come in from the various units so that we were able to get a good idea of how things had been going; with very few exceptions everything had been carried out almost according to plans, but we had been forced to pay a very heavy price. My own regiment had suffered particularly heavy losses, especially in the matter of officers. Only one of the number that had gone over the top that morning had been able to remain on duty, the other twenty-four having been wounded or killed, but fortunately in many cases the wounds had not been very serious. The one who had remained with the men was Capt. S—— and he had stuck it out all day in spite of a wound in the chest. For hours he had held on to a most precarious position, not surrendering his command until nearly midnight when he had been relieved. About 2.39 A.M. he came to the Brigade Headquarters to report and he was then in a terribly exhausted condition. With my pocket outfit I made him some tea to which a little rum was added and he has since told me that was the best drink he has ever tasted.

The rest of that night was devoted to various tasks and there was no chance for sleep or rest. Supplies and reliefs had to be sent up and reports made out and wounded men taken care of so that when morning came we were still hard at it, and a tired and somewhat dishevelled lot we were, no one having had any sleep for two nights. At six o'clock we had a sort of breakfast, and then I was sent out to see how the water supply was holding out. On my way through the lines I suddenly saw a man running along and calling out that every one must retire at once. This struck us as peculiar for retiring did not appeal to any one as the proper or correct thing, indeed we believed that advancing was far more in order. So the man was taken in charge. He was dressed as a private of the medical corps, a pale-faced fellow wearing large glasses and having a somewhat peculiar accent. His whole manner was so suspicious that it was considered advisable to send him to headquarters in custody of a corporal. What happened to him can only be conjectured but there is little doubt that he was a German who with great pluck was trying the ruse to force our men to retreat. Such acts are not rare and occasionally they succeed though more often the man who attempts it pays with his life for his audacity.

On reaching the comparatively safe valley on the edge of Bécourt Wood in which various headquarters were situated I noticed a very fine looking sergeant walking a short distance ahead of me. About a hundred yards away on the opposite side of the valley the hillside was crowded with big guns. These were firing more or less continually so that as the shells flew over our heads the noise was deafening. Suddenly the big sergeant spun round and fell. I rushed up to see what happened and found him stone dead. A piece of shell band having broken off a passing projectile had made a ghastly wound in his head.

There was nothing to be done, so I continued on my way and discovered that our shortage of water in the front line was caused by a burst pipe. Arrangements were immediately made for its repair, but in the meantime water was sadly needed so a party was organised to carry it up in petrol cans. What we would do without these useful receptacles is hard to say for their size and shape renders them of the utmost value as water carriers and even though occasionally they give to the water a taste of petrol the men put up with it readily, for after all they are accustomed to highly flavoured water as it is well purified with chloride of lime. One flavour more or less makes little difference to a thirsty, tired man.

It was nearly noon when I returned to headquarters and reported the water supply in working order. Shortly after my arrival when I had stolen a few minutes for a shave and a sort of wash some food arrived. Among the rations was a delicious ham which took my fancy for I had not had any real food since the beginning of the battle. Our dugout was so small that eating in it was out of the question so the ham was placed on a sandbag on the side of the trench; taking a knife and fork from my haversack I was about to cut a nice fat slice, but at the moment I put the fork into position a messenger came along and with due politeness I stepped back against the side of the trench which was very narrow, in order to give him room. Scarcely had he passed when with a dull sickening screech a large piece of shell casing came flying down and struck the sandbar exactly where my left wrist would have been had I continued the ham cutting operation. Besides taking my hand off it would undoubtedly have destroyed my watch, and as this had been given to me by my wife it would have been most annoying, while to have lost my hand while carving a ham would not have been very glorious. I doubt even if I could even have had the satisfaction of claiming to have been "wounded in action." For a souvenir I dug the piece of iron out of the sand bag, it having gone completely through one and partly through the second, and then I cut the ham which proved to be quite as good as it looked.

Chapter XII
Captured Lines and Prisoners

AFTER LUNCH I was told to take a party of men with rations and ammunition to be distributed among the Battalions of our Brigade which were holding the new line. Instead of going across the open of No Man's Land which was being fairly heavily shelled I was told to follow a certain new sap which led from the left of our position to the conquered trenches. This sounded quite easy, and would have been had not the Germans kept up a very unwelcome and incessant bombardment, many of the shells falling along that particular piece of trench. Snipers too were watching every shallow part of our trenches so that the greatest caution was necessary.

The whole line was blocked with dead and wounded in ghastly confusion with all sorts of débris and with shattered sand bags by the thousand. Through this mass of wreckage, human and material, we made our way slowly and painfully. Here and there I would test a particularly shallow part by holding up a "tin hat" as though a man were moving along and it always brought a rattle of bullets so it was a constant case of "low bridge." Eventually we reached the sap only to find that it was crowded to its utmost capacity with wriggling lines of men coming and going. So thickly were they packed that over an hour passed before we were able to add our number to this sweating mass. No sooner had we entered than I met the Colonel of one of our Battalions. He was lying at the entrance of a shallow dugout badly wounded, having been shot the previous morning. He begged me to get stretcher bearers for him. A splendid man he was and I would have given anything to help him but under the conditions I could not leave my party. All I could do was to send word by a passing stretcher bearer who was heroically trying to carry out a badly wounded man on his back. He was almost exhausted but promised to do his best. Later the Colonel was carried out and taken to England where I regret to say he died.

Slowly, very slowly, we moved forward while the shells dropped with disgusting persistence along the whole line, now and then making a direct hit and causing a blockade of killed and injured. It was impossible to do more than give the most hasty attention to the wounded and then prop them against the broken side of the trench for there was no room for stretcher bearers. Suddenly in the midst of the uproar came the call "German bombers are in the trench, get back as fast as you can." There was no word as to who had given the order and any attempt to go back would have been disastrous if not impossible. A regular panic was starting for the men believed themselves caught in a trap. The position demanded rapid action. Telling my party to stand fast behind me I drew my revolver and swore I would shoot the first man that moved toward me. It was a ticklish moment as the men, unnerved, and tired after the incessant work of the past two days, to say nothing of the lack of sleep, were not in condition to reason. Still the revolver made them hesitate long enough for me to ask from whom the order came. This delay saved the situation and they soon realised that no one knew where or how it had originated. I noted one man without a rifle. To be unarmed while in the front line is a crime, so I called out asking where his rifle was. He, seeing one on the ground nearby, declared that it was his and had been pushed out of his hand by the crowd. He quickly picked it up but in doing so accidentally put his finger on the trigger and a shot whizzed past my head, missing me by a few inches. Needless to say I was thoroughly frightened.

Gradually order was resumed and we once more moved forward very slowly and finally after innumerable delays reached the old German front line. Then came the question where were we to find our Battalion. For an hour we wandered about through the most thoroughly devastated piece of ground I have ever seen. Not a semblance of any trench remained, nothing but an endless succession of craters of every size; as though there were not enough still more were constantly being made by the Germans who were shelling the region with great persistence. Various groups of men told us just where our lot were to be found but all the information proved valueless and simply led to our doing a lot of hard walking and climbing. Finally I left the men to rest for they were heavily loaded with supplies and taking a couple of N.C.O.'s[5] with me went on a tour of investigation. The only result was that from one point we had a splendid view of the storming of the shattered village of La Boisselle. This was of the greatest interest for we could see how well our men did their work. Yet to see how the lines were thinned by the terrific machine-gun fire made one feel utterly sick.

After dodging a few shells and nearly getting lost in the labyrinth of craters, I succeeded in getting back to my party. They had almost decided to start off on their own account, imagining that I had been "scuppered" (the vernacular for killed) for I had been gone such a long time. As far as we could see there was no hope of finding the remains of our Battalions to which we were trying to bring supplies. Every landmark was obliterated by the long continued bombardment.

The German system of trenches, which I firmly believed I knew thoroughly, no longer existed, in its place there was only an endless array of craters of all sizes, with here and there the remains of a dugout the entrance to which was in most cases filled with mangled bodies torn beyond belief. Some of these were still wearing gas protecting helmets, showing that they had been caught by our gas attack of the 26th. Nothing more grotesque or horrible can be imagined than these figures, black or yellow from the effects of different poisonous gases, and wearing the masks. The protruding retainers hung from their mouths and gave them the appearance of some hideous animal.

In the craters were numerous bodies exposed or partly buried, both Germans and our own men, showing how severe the fighting had been. Several of the Germans still clutched in their stiff cold hands rifles, to which were attached the saw-edged bayonet, and on the teeth of some

---

5. Non-commissioned officer, i.e., any one above the rank of private and below the rank of Second Lieutenant.

of these barbarous weapons was the proof that they are used for other purposes than the cutting of wood. The Boche claims that they belong to the pioneers and are not used in fighting, but the claim bears as much relation to truth as some of his other statements which he hoped the world would swallow.

While we were trying to discover the whereabouts of our lost units the enemy began a very unpleasant *strafe*. Shell after shell landed around us and made the task of moving about decidedly risky, I might even say dangerous. It is one thing to have to cross a shelled zone and go straight from one point to another, but to wander about crawling in and out of craters, being sniped wherever you exposed your anatomy in getting out of one crater and into another, and expecting a five-inch or larger shell to be your boon companion when you got snugly into the crater, while you know the men you are looking for are carefully hidden, well, it is not quite as nice as you may think, in fact I can honestly say that I was frightened and the incessant noise of bursting shells was head-splitting.

After various disagreeable things had happened, things about which one simply cannot write, I decided to return and try later on to get the supplies delivered under the cover of night. It was easy enough to make this decision but quite another thing to carry it out. The communication trench, or sap, through which we had come was being shelled more vigorously than ever, and if possible it was even more crowded. Unfortunately it was the only available cover; to have gone out in the open would have been neither more nor less than suicide, as the Boches still held the opposite slope of Sausage Valley where they had a number of machine guns. These raked every inch of No Man's Land in this neighbourhood. The fact that they were there was due to a slight mistake that had occurred the previous day. Steps were being taken, in the form of a large bombing party, to stamp out the hornets' nest that night. I may add that it succeeded quite thoroughly, so much so that not a single German escaped. Bombs of the Mill's grenade kind form exceedingly convincing arguments.

Eventually we managed to make our way back to H. Q. dugout and

I reported my complete failure. This was not a pleasant task, it hurt my pride worse than anything I have ever done. The Brigadier was extremely nice about it and said he fully understood the difficulties. Another try was to be made that evening when things might be more quiet.

There was very good news from most parts of the line that night, Fricourt, the much dreaded strong point which our men had partly surrounded, had fallen, the Germans having been forced to abandon it. La Boisselle also had been taken, and Shelter Wood after many attempts was at last in our hands.

According to the German report which appeared later they were retiring "according to plan." This was perfectly true, but in the official explanation of the great retreat which continued for weeks they quite forgot to mention who made the plan. Need I add, *we made it?*

The night passed fairly quietly, evidently both the Germans and our men were tired after the two severe days, and beyond intermittent shelling and a few very half-hearted counter attacks there was practically no offensive activity. Our men spent the time consolidating our newly acquired lines and bringing up supplies of food and ammunition.

One day, I forget which, there was a rather amusing incident connected with the carrying of ammunition. Hand grenades were badly needed in a certain part, and some bright fellow thought it would be a splendid plan to make use of a batch of freshly captured German prisoners. So he marched them down to a forward supply dump and loaded them up with canvas buckets full of Mill's grenades. As I recall it there were about thirty men, accompanied by a guard of four of our fellows who marched them across No Man's Land toward our new line. The plan was a curious one and would have succeeded had not some senior officer discovered it. He was highly indignant. The employment of prisoners for such purpose being entirely contrary to rules and regulations. Had those prisoners possessed a proper amount of self-sacrificing patriotism they could have played havoc, armed as they were with some forty grenades apiece. That they would eventually have been killed it is needless to say, and evidently that pleasant prospect was in their minds, for a more docile crew I have never seen. As one of the guards said, "Why bless yer, sir, they'd just eat out of yer 'and they're so bloomin' glad to be safe."

They were a tired looking outfit, dirty and untidy and many were in a terrible nervous condition. They declared the bombardment to which they had been subjected was more than human beings could stand and as already stated their water supply and food had been used up, and it had been impossible to bring up fresh supplies owing to the incessant shelling. Occasionally a couple of men had managed to make their way back for supplies, but in most cases they were knocked out either going or coming, very rarely did one return. One of the men spoke English perfectly. He had been a waiter in a certain well-known restaurant in London. He asked what we were doing over there, and exhibited a photograph showing London completely destroyed by Zeppelins. It was a good fake and the man was much surprised when he heard that so far as the eye could see London had in no way changed since his departure. The Hun has a funny way of keeping up the national enthusiasm. He quite forgets that people have memories, and that occasionally they do reason things out. About a year later, that is in 1917, after one of the big air raids over London the people were informed that the metropolis was practically destroyed. This was most complimentary to us for apparently we are credited with being able to build with unheard-of speed.

For fear that the German soldier will give himself up too readily they are told frightful tales about what we do to prisoners. We are supposed to first inflict untold tortures on them with the idea of eliciting information regarding military matters, and then, having amused ourselves in this way we put them to death.

These are among the many pleasant things we do, and strange to say the wretched creatures in a number of cases believe most implicitly that these stories are true. We often find them offering bribes to our men, watches, money and other things if only their lives may be spared. They appeal to our men's sympathy by showing photographs of their wives and children, explaining how painful it will be for them if they never return.

In one case a poor shell-shocked Boche, one among a batch that was being led by a somewhat diminutive cockney, adorned with red hair, a freckled face and a snub nose which pointed heavenward. Not at all the hero type so far as appearance goes. The Boche after offering one by one all his valuables and receiving each time only a shake of the head and the remark "Nothin' doin'" finally handed his iron cross as though certain that this particular individual of the Thomas Atkins family could not resist such a tempting bribe. T. A. took it in his hand and the doleful Boche actually allowed a smile of sorts to crawl over his gloomy face, but the smile died a sudden death when the little cockney handed back the cross with the remark, "'Ere, take it back, old son, yer jolly well won it, didn't yer?" This flabbergasted the Teuton who thought the brutal British had doomed him to certain death. What a surprise it must have been to him and to all the others when they found how thoroughly well they were treated.

People laugh at us, and call us soft, because we err on the side of *over*-kindness to our prisoners, regardless of the terrible provocation we have had to retaliate on them for the brutal way in which they have so often behaved to our poor chaps, but in the end our actions will undoubtedly produce greater and more far-reaching results. These tens of thousands that we have captured will spread stories when they are released which will help vastly in making us better understood throughout the whole world.

Our men greatly prefer to fight in a clean sportsman-like way, and the ill treating or killing of prisoners "spoils the fun of fighting," as they say; but unfortunately the only too numerous examples of German treachery when captured, have forced our men to act in a way which would never be necessary if we were fighting an honourable foe.

An instance which occurred to our men on the Somme the first day of the battle will give an idea of what we are contending with. It happened when our fellows were clearing a trench (this means seeing that every dugout and hiding place has been cleared of the enemy). They came to a deep dugout and called down the stairway for surrender. The dugout contained some twenty men and officers, who replied that they gave themselves up. Our Yorkshire men are not fools and so they prepared against treachery, two held short-fuse grenades in readiness, while the other four stood by with rifles, also in readiness.

Up came the Huns carrying no weapons and with hands held up in the required position. About eighteen men all told and our fellows, thinking this was the lot, were about to march the batch away, when suddenly two German officers sprang out of the dugout with automatic pistols. These they proceeded to use, but our good men were equal to the occasion and two grenades quickly dropped among the treacherous brutes and then two more to make sure, with the result that our men were not encumbered with any prisoners.

Now such behaviour on the part of the Germans is bound to produce very disagreeable effects and they are quite certain to be the sufferers, but certainly they have no one but themselves to blame. It is needless to add that our fellows decided not to waste much time when they came to the next dugout. Being decent meant taking quite unnecessary risks, and when a risk is unnecessary a soldier is not justified in taking it.

I could not help remarking on how very thoroughly the remaining dugouts were cleared. People may hold up their hands in righteous horror at this cold-blooded performance but before doing so let them consider what their feelings would have been had some of these men of ours been their own relations, brothers, fathers or husbands, and remember that had they not been both clever and very quick every one would have been treacherously killed. It is bad enough to lose ones kith and kin in regular fighting when all must take their chance, but to be killed by men, brutes perhaps would be the better word, whose lives you have honourably spared is quite different, and we must not judge our men harshly if they do occasionally administer punishment for some dastardly deed of cowardly treachery and inhuman cruelty. When they do have the chance to fight cleanly and fairly they do so, thank God.

In the meantime the reader having kindly pardoned this digression we will return to our ammunition carrying prisoners.

The supply of grenades was carefully stored in a safe place to await the arrival of a fatigue (work) party and the batch of prisoners once more turned their backs on the field of battle; each step took them further from the chance of being killed by indiscriminate shells which insisted on falling in unexpected and quite unnecessary places. Thoughtlessly enough the men showed their feelings of relief. They smiled, and that was foolish, for it gave a brilliant idea to their guarding angel, to himself he said "Prisoners must not be employed in carrying ammunition, that's right enough, but the blighters can be put to the very useful task of carrying water for the poor beggars who are so busy in the front line, good idea that's what they'll do," and they did, and no one got into a row about it. I think it is quite safe to say that no water ever tasted sweeter to our men than that chlorinated, petrolated, warm water carried to them by the Boche prisoners. As one fellow remarked as he drank "to the Kaiser's 'ealth in 'ell," "It's the nectar of the gods."

Chapter XIII
The Toll of Battle

DURING THE MORNING of the 3rd there was no special work for me to do for an hour or two so I employed myself searching for wounded men, many of whom had been laying out in the open for over two days.

During any big "push" there is bound to be this unfortunate delay in picking up the wounded, it is unavoidable. The number that fall is so large that it completely overwhelms the stretcher bearers who work to the very limit of their power. All lightly wounded men who can possibly manage it are asked to make their way as best they can to the nearest dressing station, but there are vast numbers who cannot walk, and who must therefore await assistance. These poor fellows have a way of crawling into shell holes for safety so that they are hidden, and it is difficult to discover them. Then also if badly injured they keep so quiet that they are easily mistaken for the dead with which in this great battle the ground was strewn, as far as the eye could see. Nearly every one of these bodies must be examined and the stretcher bearers were so terribly overworked that many a badly wounded man necessarily must be passed for dead during the earlier hurried examinations.

No words can give any adequate idea of the splendid work of the stretcher bearer. No praise is too high for him. He has none of the excitement of those who fight, none of the glory of wresting trenches from the enemy. His is the hard, gruesome, yet wonderful work of mercy. No sooner has a "show" begun than he is needed, and from then on he must not stop, day and night. In the comparative shelter of trenches or in the shell-swept open, facing danger without a thought for his own safety, his one idea is to find those who have fallen, and by some method get them back to the dressing station.

Often it is impossible to move the wounded man, then the stretcher bearer does what he can to dress the wound and make the sufferer as comfortable as possible. To friend and foe the same treatment is given. Once a man is down, his nationality makes no difference, but when possible the wise and careful stretcher bearer removes any weapons from within the reach of the wounded German. For sad experience has taught the lesson that many a one that has been wounded after having been bound up by our fellows has returned good for evil by shooting his benefactors in the back.

Those who have never seen the stretcher bearer at work can have no idea of the difficulties he encounters. Carrying men who are *acting* the part of the wounded in beautiful symmetrical home-made practice trenches appears so easy, but to carry a really wounded man through irregular shell torn trenches, which are perhaps crowded with moving troops or strewn with wounded and dead, is a task that calls for untiring strength and patience. The fact that a few minutes' delay may make all the difference in the man's chance of being saved, adds a nervous strain which cannot be described.

During the two hours I had to spare this morning there was a good opportunity of seeing the wonderful work of the S.Bs and as I did what I could to help, my admiration became greater and greater. Some of the sights were too ghastly to be spoken of, but one thing above all others which impressed itself on me was the truly heroic patience and pluck of the wounded, seldom a groan, never a complaint and usually a murmured word of thanks for any help they received; and people dare to say that war brutalises men. I thank God that I have seen what men can be, for I have never known it in peace time, and I say, without fear of contradiction (and I do not count the contradiction of the stay-at-homes, they do not know), that the very finest that is in a man is developed *out there*. The callous gain hearts, yes, great big hearts. The soft-hearted suffer. Lord how they suffer, but their suffering becomes unselfish. They swallow their own agonies as they help the poor mutilated beings that so often have lost all resemblance to men. Perhaps at home these soft-hearted super-sensitive men, and there are plenty such, would be called *faint-*hearted. They might not allow themselves to help an injured creature for fear of harrowing their own delicate feelings. That selfishness vanishes *out there*. They become men. Is that brutalising? No indeed, it is just the reverse. One becomes accustomed to death, for worse luck one sees so much of it. A poor dead body is not a thing to shudder at or be afraid of, but that does not mean that we become callous. We no longer look on death as such a terrible thing, nor on our puny selves as being so all-important. Our sense of proportion becomes more true, and we are more likely to see ourselves as we really are, important only to our own immediate friends and relations. We become more humble and surely that is good for us.

Some people say that because our men sing and joke while on their way to that scientific slaughter ground, the modern battlefield, that they have no religion, that they are materialists. They do not know the hearts of these men, they have not seen them during their only too brief leisure hours in the days before the battle go quietly into the little churches and silently offer up their simple prayers. Is it for themselves they pray? I doubt it. No, it is for those at home, for wives and kiddies, and for mothers who are thinking of them so many miles away. There is more real religion out there near the line of battle than is ever seen at home. It is not ostentation, but quiet, deep and beautifully sincere.

Not long ago I met a young man, a civilian, who was filled with the desire to help *others* to be better. He was of the anaemic type in both body and mind. He lacked all experience in the great busy world that is doing things, and had never been two hundred miles from home. He came to me and asked my advice about an idea that he had. I was anxious to hear what his idea might be for the complete lack of expression in his face made me think that an idea and himself could scarcely be related. It turned out that he wanted to go to France to *uplift* the wicked soldiers. He was quite upset when I pointed out that those men out there were doing far more than he was. That they were following Christ's example in offering their lives for the good of others, ready at any moment to make the Supreme Sacrifice. That generally speaking they were living honest clean lives, on the average far better than civilians at home, and finally, that if he wanted to do missionary work he would find his field without going to France.

Now why should people imagine that we poor soldiers are so much worse than any one else? Why should all sorts of laws be made to protect civilians from our evil influence as though we were moral lepers? We are even denied some of the privileges accorded to the slacker who stays at home and grows fat on his ill-gotten gains. We are actually punished because we are shouldering the burden of military service. This is very hard for us to understand. For when we see what the soldiers do, even though they are but temporary soldiers, who have given up civilian pursuits to "do their bit," one cannot help feeling that they are certainly no worse than those who stay at home, and that the effect of the war on them is refining rather than brutalising. They will come out of it better men in every way, broader minded and more charitable and very much more sympathetic, besides having learned a great many things which will be of the utmost value to them in life.

Details of what happened during our search for the wounded cannot be given. Sometimes the scenes were only too painfully pathetic and again they were sadly amusing, if that combination can be imagined, but the less badly injured would often make such absurdly humorous remarks that it was impossible not to laugh. One fellow had no less than three wounds - his right shoulder, his left hand, and his thigh. He had managed to wriggle into a shell hole for safety he said as he was "afraid of getting hit"; but once in the crater he could not get out. In describing his predicament he said that never before had he realised how hard it was to roll up hill. But that is not what bothered him, his trouble was that he could not get at his "fags" (cigarettes). They were in his pocket, but owing to the hand and arm being injured he was unable to reach them. As the S.B. was binding his wounds preparatory to moving him he remarked in most approved cockney "Blime me, old chap, but if I ever catches that bounder what put that there last shot into my left 'and, I'm blowed if I wouldn't jest knock 'is bloomin' blitherin' fice (face) in so that 'is own pot-beliied German father wouldn't recognise 'is lawful horf-spring. I wouldn't er minded t'other two blarsted pills, but me fags is all in me pocket, four packs o' blessed Woodbines what me company hofficer gave me, and 'ere I been two mortal dies (days) and not a bloomin' smoke. Its a bleedin' shime I says, come on 'ere, like a good chap, and put *two* in me mouth to make up for lost time - that's the ticket, Oh Gawd but that's a bit of orl right (as the cigarettes were put in his mouth and lighted) 'ere 'ave one, or two. Th're just like kids and beer two's better 'n one any toime. Ah 'old on a bit there (as they lifted him on to a stretcher) that old leg's napoo[6] its got ther toothache or somethin', jest pick her up by both ends."

But the pain was more than he could stand in his weakened condition and he went off in a dead faint. The cigarettes were taken from his colourless lips, "pinched out," and tucked in orthodox fashion behind his ears, ready for him when he regained consciousness. I watched the poor fellow being carried off and marvelled at his courage and spirits, not even a word of complaint at the long wait before help had come.

Turning in the opposite direction I scanned the many motionless khaki figures which lay around me in such curious positions; if one looked at them steadily they seemed to move, and several times I was about to start for one when I realised from its attitude that it was one of the Supreme Sacrifices. About a hundred yards away there was a patch of glowing scarlet poppies. They fascinated me, their cheerful colour in the field of death, as though nature laughed at our mourning. As I stared something moved very slightly, so slightly indeed that I thought I must be mistaken and I was about to move away, but an unknown power seemed to lead me forward to the poppies in spite of myself, and I made my way over the shell torn, body-strewn, ground. On arriving I found a badly wounded man, he was lying in the poppy patch and with one arm extended so that the hand was out in the open. What I had seen was the fingers moving, but it had been enough, perhaps, to save the man's life. The flowers so completely surrounded him that very likely he would never have been found, except perhaps by the burial party.

---

6. i.e., no good, "nothing doing" - derived (more or less) from the French Il n'y en a plus.

So far the morning had been fairly quiet in this particular neighbourhood, very few shells having fallen in our immediate vicinity, though innumerable machine gun bullets sang through the air overhead, and in the distance toward Mametz Wood and Contalmaison there was the unceasing pounding of the big guns. Evidently the Germans were disputing every yard of our advance, but our men were pushing forward with splendid determination. It was gratifying to learn later that in no place had an enemy counter- attack been successful for more than a short time.

As I was about to return to H.Q.[7] our Roman Catholic Padre passed me. He was on his way to where the greatest number of our men had fallen not far from the German front line of three days ago. Up to the moment there had been no time or opportunity for burying the dead, nor was there much chance that it would be done for some days to come,[8] and it appeared that our Brigade had just received orders to move back for reorganisation. Our good Padre could not bear to think that a strange priest would read the service over his "boys" as he called them. The boys he had lived with for over two years. How often he had scolded them for their little failings, and now so many lay before him - their ears deaf to the human voice, their great strong bodies stiff, cold and inert. He had loved them with a great devotion and many a one, torn and bleeding, had he carried off the field on his powerful shoulders utterly regardless of the passing bullets. He was a great man, admired by all who knew him, whether Catholic or not. (I regret to say that some months later he was badly wounded while carrying a message under terrific fire, a task that he had voluntarily assumed.) On that battlefield of the Somme he stood, exposed to the shells which were coming in increasing number, and there silhouetted against the sky-line, I saw him read the burial service consigning the dead to eternal rest, not individually, but in hundreds, yes thousands. It was impressive in its simplicity and it touched the hearts of all who witnessed it.

---

7. Head Quarters.
8. It was actually about twelve days before the burying began.

On returning to H.Q. I learned that we were to leave at eight o'clock and go to D——t where we expected to entrain for a place far back from the scene of the great conflict. The news was welcome for we were tired out, a long rest was needed and had certainly been well-earned by the men.

In the afternoon I asked permission to go forward to see if I could find poor B——'s (the Brigade Major) body and rescue if possible any of his belongings to send home to his family. His servant, who like every one else had been devoted to him, was completely broken down by the loss, and he begged permission to accompany me. He thought that between us we might bring back the body and have it properly buried.

After some little trouble we succeeded in making our way across the ground between our old line and the sunken road. What a scene of desolation it presented! More utter and complete destruction could not be imagined. No sign of the original German trenches remained, and our men were busily engaged in digging new lines of communication and putting up barbed wire entanglements in anticipation of the inevitable counter-attacks. Beyond us lay Fricourt, or more properly what had been Fricourt, for it was now nothing but a mass of smouldering ruin; not a wall was standing, the very bricks were broken into fragments. Where trees had stood, there remained only the torn and splintered stumps, but no words can describe the completeness of the ruin. The sunken road along which only a few days before the Germans had so confidently driven their supply carts and marched their men, was now more of shell-holes than road; shattered limbers, waggons and guns, distorted remains of horses and men, were strewn in endless confusion, while our men crouched into hastily constructed trenches along the road side and dodged the cursed shells. The enemy knew we should be using this road and he made us pay heavy toll. As we walked along, between the extreme bursts of hate, three men went ahead of us laughing and joking in the usual way. A single shell landed on the road just ahead of I them. Two of the men spun round like tops and then fell dead. The third was not touched. "Close shave that," he remarked as we passed him.

On the left side of the road there were two small patches of woods called the Dingle and Round Wood. These, before the big bombardment, had contained trees, but now scarcely even stumps remained, so thoroughly had they been shelled. Scattered thickly among the connecting shell holes were great numbers of bodies, both German and British. Among the dead were some wounded, very few, because the constant fire, both before and after our men had captured the ground, had finished off nearly all who had fallen. During the advance probably hundreds of our fellows had crept or rushed over this piece of territory in trying to reach the comparative shelter afforded by the eastern bank of the Sunken Road, but somewhere in Round Wood lay a German sniper, a man of great courage and persistence, who felt it his particular duty to pick off any man, or more particularly, officer, who came along the road.

He made our progress most uneven and difficult. I might say hazardous, for he was not much over a hundred yards away and so it was easy for him to send bullets unpleasantly close to our heads; only by going forward by bounds and zig-zags could we hope to avoid hitting those persistent bullets. Judging from the somewhat erratic shooting of our friend I should say he was wounded, and not in a very comfortable position, at least not in position really favourable for good marksmanship, but still I could not help admiring the fellow's pluck. Evidently he had pretended to be dead when our men were anywhere near him, and then when opportunity offered he had probably shot them in the back. To have got the man would have been very desirable, but to distinguish him among the mass of figures would be by no means an easy task. Only by very careful stalking, which would require a lot of time, would there have been any chance of getting him, and we were in a hurry; already more than half of my allotted time had passed, so we hurried forward, dodging trouble until at length we discovered the body of our friend.

Of course he was dead. That I had expected, but he had been stripped of everything of value, watch, glasses and all. This was a sad meeting of the living and the dead and I could not help thinking of the idiotic remarks one so often hears by the jealous and the armchair critics regarding the "Staff." That they stick in safe places and do nothing but make mistakes, and never take the risks they arrange for others. How sick it makes one to hear the drivel of such fools.

Perhaps we in our Division were unusually fortunate but certainly our Staff never shirked any job because it was dangerous, on the contrary they might invariably be found in the places where there was the greatest possible danger. When the attack began where was the Brigade Headquarters, back in the zone of safety? Not much, it was within a biscuit throw of the actual front line trench and the Brigadier did not hide in a safe trench and get *reports* of what was going on. He stood on the top of the parapet, and saw with his own eyes what was happening, taking no notice whatever of the hail of bullets that passed him, and here was poor B——, he had gone *forward* of any of our positions, and given his splendid life, doing even more than his duty. We could not carry the body back, to have done so would have been suicide, but I enclosed in a bottle where it would be safe from rain, a paper giving his rank, name and unit, with the instructions that his grave should not be unmarked, and so we left him and made our way back to H.Q. in time to attend to various duties incidental to our departure.

Chapter XIV
Rest - and Return to the "Show"

AT EIGHT O'CLOCK we left, tired through and through and looking forward to the quiet of the land-of-no-guns. Through lack of sleep and the continued strain my nerves were in a very ragged state. This led me to do something for which I felt most deeply ashamed. As we walked over the open shell-torn ground, occasional bullets flew past us, most of them a long way off, but one came perhaps thirty or forty feet over my head and I *ducked*. The act was almost unconscious, and no one knows the mortification I experienced when the Brigadier, who was only a few yards behind me, laughed and said, "You're slow, Dugmore; that bullet had passed long before you ducked." I wished at the time that another bullet would come and bestow on me the order of the R.I.P.

It was a forlorn looking lot that made their way to D——t. Yet though battle weary, dirty and footsore, the men wore an air of keen satisfaction. They had been tried, and they had not been found wanting. The work had been allotted, and they had done all that flesh and blood could do, and now before them was rest, wonderful rest in a peaceful part of the country, miles and miles from the front. It was something to which they could look forward with pleasure. Occasionally as they marched they would look back, and seeing the ruddy glow of shell-fire in the darkening sky they made pitying remarks on the hard luck of the "poor blighters" who were still in the fight.

Shortly after eleven our camping site was reached. It was a bare open field. The camp cookers for all the four Battalions were lined up ready with good hot food for all hands, delicious solid food and steaming hot tea. What a meal that was! and the supply was more than abundant, for our ranks were sadly thinned. Scarcely was the meal eaten than great drops of rain splashed down from the overcast sky, but no one cared. The men were fed, and they did not have to fight; what more could they ask? Within a few minutes the ground was covered with lines of men rolled in their waterproof ground sheets, sleeping the sleep of complete exhaustion, while the rain fell in torrents. That we had no pillows or mattresses or tents made no difference, all that was wanted was the chance to sleep and *forget*. Yes above all *forget*.

At four o'clock the bugle sounded, and men stretched and yawned, and cursed the disturbing call. It was not yet daylight, but the rain had stopped, and it did not seem as though they had been asleep more than a few minutes. Some of us washed, a few shaved, and all had breakfast. Then came the long wait for the train. It was due to come for us at six, but not until nine o'clock did we start. The long time had been spent in trying to find out news of our different friends whose faces did not appear in the lines, but most of the information received was unreliable. In the excitement and confusion of a big advance very little is seen, and very much is imagined. Even the roll-call did not give a very accurate idea of our losses for men might yet turn up. Many become separated from their units and do not turn up for days and even weeks. All that we knew for certain was that the Brigade had suffered very heavily, how heavily we scarcely dared think.

By slow stages we travelled all day, the train taking us to within a few miles of our preliminary destination. Here we were to tidy up and await the General's inspection. There was no more scouting work to do for the present and as my old Battalion had lost nearly all of its officers, including the Colonel, I went back to it as second in command until it was settled whether our Major was to be given command, or whether a new Colonel would be appointed. Needless to say we were anxious to get our men in shape for the General who was due on the 6th, so all our spare time was devoted to cleaning up.

On the morning of the 6th we marched to a fine old country place which was loaned for the occasion. The grounds at first glance seemed absurdly small, and I was beginning to wonder how it would be possible to arrange the four Battalions when the sad fact dawned on me that we no longer required a large space. After a slight delay we adjusted ourselves to the new conditions and the poor old Brigade was drawn up. How it had dwindled! In the old days we had made such a fine showing with our four thousand men, and now, more than half of them had failed to respond when their names were called. On the General's arrival we formed into a square and listened to the words of thanks for what had been done. I had often heard or read of what a first inspection after a battle means but never had I realised what a painful experience it could be. Men swallowed hard and avoided each other's eyes for many of the eyes were moist.

That same night word came that we would move the following morning to Le M——e a short day's march and once there we would receive our reinforcements and spend a month or six weeks getting into shape. This sounded delightful, but like most cheerful promises it did not come true.

On arriving at our new quarters we were delighted to find a peaceful little country hamlet in the midst of a beautiful country. A perfect place in which to recuperate. The billets were quite good, and we settled down to make ourselves as comfortable as possible, and amused ourselves reading accounts of the Battle of the Somme as they appeared in the newspapers.

Having read the various stories we came to the conclusion quite unanimously that we had not taken part in the "Show," had not even been there - and further we doubted if there had been anything more than a series of skirmishes, just a slight variety to the ordinary daily monotony of trench warfare. Our conceit was taken out of us and we felt exceedingly humble.

The day of the 8th was given up to rest and getting everything arranged. The following morning there was to be an inspection of kit and drawing of whatever was necessary to make up the inevitable deficiencies, for in battle much is lost. In the afternoon we were notified that a new Colonel was coming, and late that evening he arrived. This meant of course that I would no longer be second in command, so much to my delight it was arranged that I should take my old company or rather what was left of it.

Things happen quickly out in France, and the next afternoon the Colonel announced that we were to return to the front the following morning. The order was in the form of a letter, the purport of which was that as the Brigade had done so splendidly *The Higher Command felt that it was only due to it (the Brigade) that another opportunity for distinguishing itself should be given and the said Higher Command felt complete confidence in the work that the Brigade would do, etc., etc.* This we had to read out to the men. It caused a sad and cynical smile and I fear that all of us felt somewhat rebellious and greatly disappointed. It did not seem fair to the men, they needed a rest, and then we had lost all our sergeant-majors and most of our sergeants the entire internal organisation had to be readjusted. We had scarcely any officers and they were mostly new fellows who had no experience at the front, and finally we were below half strength. To get into the "Show" under such conditions would not give the Brigade half a chance. It is true that new drafts were promised before we reached the front line, but it requires some time to assimilate new men, and as far as we could see the time could not be given to us.

On the morning of the 10th we left our rest billets and said good-bye somewhat sadly to Le M——e. A good half day's marching brought us to A——s where we were to take the train, but something had gone wrong both with the train and the rations and we had to wait till late that night. The only food was what we bought out of our own pockets. We scoured the village and had to perform a sort of barley loaves and little fish miracle, but the fragments left would not have filled many baskets. Scarcely a particle of bread or chocolate was left in that village. We had acted like the locusts of Egypt, but unlike them we left money in full (very full I should say) payment. Eventually the train arrived and took us to V——e our old stamping ground. The distance was only a few miles, but many hours, very weary hours, were occupied in the journey.

Soon after our arrival we received the new drafts. Men of many different regiments, some had been in the attack of July 1st, others were new arrivals who had not seen a trench, and it was a merry task sorting and arranging the lot. In fact the day was one of the busiest I have ever seen, rolls had to be made up, gas helmets tested, kits inspected, deficiencies made good, iron rations issued[9], new N.C.O.s appointed and a thousand and one things to be done. Some new officers having come to add to the confusion, they had to be sized up and allotted to companies. It was midnight before we were able to get a chance to sleep and the orders were that we should proceed to Bottom Wood, beyond Fricourt the following morning.

Any old soldier would have been amused had he seen us getting ready to move. The battalion had to be drawn up and roughly inspected, and owing to the restricted area it was necessary to move the companies about more or less. Being a *Light Infantry* regiment we have many pecularities as to drill and orders. One item being that the men are not called to attention and given the *"slope 'ums,"* preparatory to moving, we simply say "move to the right (or left) in fours. Form fours - right" and off they go, springing to attention automatically as the first part of the move and marching off at the "trail." Fully half of our new men knew nothing of our Light Infantry idiosyncrasies, and were completely lost. The idea of being expected to move without being called to attention or given the "slope" was too much for them. The result was one grand and very glorious confusion, for which no one was to blame. At first our Colonel, who was a regular from a Highland Light Infantry regiment, and a splendid fellow, accustomed to having things done strictly according to rules and regulations, gazed with indignation and rapidly rising temper at the horrible muddle. A word whispered in his ear at the critical moment explained the situation and discipline or no discipline there was a suppressed giggle before the mongrel Battalion finally got under way with more or less uniformity of action.

Our march to Bottom Wood was decidedly interesting but slow, owing

---

9. Emergency rations, not to be used except by officer's order.

to the enormous amount of traffic on the road. There are few things that give a better idea of the magnitude of modern war than the road traffic, the never ceasing stream of moving war supplies. For the 24 hours of each day, the seven days of each week it goes on like the driving belt of a monster machine, - the belt that operates this colossal instrument of war. Needless to say the handling of this vast mass of moving material requires the most perfect organisation. Not only must the starting of each item be regulated with absolute precision, but its destination, even in the midst of a battle where the elements of uncertainty are so great, must be equally well planned. And then the roads themselves which are subject to the terrific wear and tear as well as the destruction by shells must be maintained in perfect condition, repairs being made with the least possible delay. To insure smooth working of the whole traffic system members of the military traffic squad are stationed at intervals along the roads and at the crossings to see that everything shall move according to plan.

Passing us there was every type of conveyance, from giant, indomitable caterpillar tractors, to hand carts - carrying every imaginable article used in this modern warfare, from huge shells that looked big enough to wipe out the whole German army, to bales of innocent hay for the horses. Sandwiched in between these various transports were units of every branch of the service, artillery, cavalry and poor weary "foot sloggers" as we infantry are called.

This great endless caravan, carrying forward its unmeasurable weight of man and material with slow resistless power, was a sight to inspire, and it gave fresh courage and hope to the tired men. Against this moving mass, returning from the land of shells and horrors, were the "empties" going back to be refilled, for the maw of battle is never satisfied, never filled; and then there were the endless ambulances bearing in their covered bodies the price of our victories, and our men looked with envy on the pale bandaged figures who were bound for the wonderful hospitals where all that human kindness can do is done, where men learn to understand and appreciate women, those women who bear the blessed symbol of the Cross of Red and devote their energies and their great sympathies to the merciful work of healing. It is scarcely to be wondered at that our men were envious of these "Blighties."

On either side of the road the fields were massed with men and material, and one could not help thinking of the change that a few days had made. Less than two weeks ago this was a shell-swept area, and now it was a huge encampment. As we continued the changes were still more noticeable, and still more satisfactory. For as we entered Fricourt we passed what remained of the railway station in which stood the riddled and wrecked remnants of the last train that had moved over that line almost two years ago, and now our engineers were clearing the line and making ready to relay the tracks for the trains which would very soon be running into the station. And Fricourt itself! What a scene it presented not only of destruction but construction. Already the main road had been cleared of débris and repaired sufficiently to allow of its being used. Dugouts were made habitable and wire entanglements erected for defensive purposes. The whole place was seething with activity, and it did one good to think that never again would the Germans set foot in the village they had occupied for so long. No one knew what a satisfaction it was to us to note all these things and to realise that our men had played so large a part in bringing about this great change.[10]

The sight of this evidence of our gains had a wonderful effect on the spirits of our men, and they went forward with a new spring in their step. On we went keeping to the right of Fricourt Wood and continued till we reached Bottom Wood where the Battalion was distributed according to plan. My company held the line on the north eastern edge of the wood and a rough piece of trench it was, much of it had been completely destroyed by shells and the whole place was littered with all sorts of war material, rifles, bombs, clothing, accoutrement of all kind, food and so forth, most of which was German.

Fortunately there were not very many bodies lying about. Of course the few we found had to be buried without delay as they had been there many days. While some of the men were engaged in this unpleasant

---

10. Alas Fricourt has recently been retaken by the Germans.

task the others were set to consolidating the trench, and clearing the parts that had fallen in. This also proved far from agreeable as many naked bodies were unearthed. The Germans with their high degree of efficiency and lack of sentiment remove everything from their dead. So the finding of these bodies was gruesome, to express it in mildest terms.

For three days we occupied the line, and they were three days of misery as the enemy kept up a regular rain of lachrymatory gas shells so that every crater was a reservoir of the vile stuff and the very ground itself was impregnated with it. The result was that we were in a constant state of crying, for the gas, so well named "tear gas" causes intense inflammation of the eyes as well as to the membrane of the throat and nose. Fortunately it is not deadly, but it makes life a miserable burden and results in a great loathing for the very name of a German. For a short time the goggles with which we are furnished, act as a protection, but it is not long before the gas gets through and attacks the eyes.

During our spare time, when things were quiet, we collected and sorted all material that had any value, so that when the salvage company came it could be easily handled.

Chapter XV
A Hot Corner - Gassed

ON THE EVENING of the 14th we received the orders, for which we had been waiting, rumour, that unreliable source of trouble, had said that after all we should not be needed and so we half expected to return to finish our disturbed rest. But no such luck! Our orders were to move forward at six the following morning to a given point at the south east corner of Mametz Wood, where we should find the rest of the Brigade, and further instruction would be sent later.

On the morning of the 15th I assembled my company preparatory to moving, while going over the line to see that everything was left in proper order and that my ex-German dugout contained nothing in the way of papers. I heard a shell making its way toward me with entirely unnecessary speed. Frankly I thought it was going to hit me, but no, it fell some thirty yards or so directly in front, I crouched low, expecting it to burst, but instead of the orthodox deafening roar, there was only a mild *puff*. Dud, thought I, and thanked the careless person who had presumably made some mistake in the shell's makeup. I was premature in the congratulations and thanks, for apparently the shell contained phosgene gas, which up to then was entirely new to us. Owing to the pollution of the air by the omnipresent pineapple-smelling tear gas, I could not detect the odour of the new poison, and the thick fog which prevailed at the time prevented the gas from spreading freely.

This probably saved me from a bad dose, and at the time beyond an increased irritation of the throat and a disagreeable shortness of breath I did not feel the effects.

As we were about to start, a Battalion of one of the Scottish regiments passed us; as they disappeared into the fog with their kilts swinging to their long slow strides, I could not help thinking what a fine body of men they were. The kilts make them appear abnormally tall and sturdy. As soon as they had cleared us we moved toward the sound of the guns; at first we had to trust to the compass for our direction, but gradually the fog lifted and as we reached what was known with such good reason as Death's Valley Road, a large body of troops came along. I halted my company and waited for the column to pass, since we were well ahead of tune. Scarcely had it gone a hundred yards clear of us than we heard the dreaded hum of a huge shell coming and an instant later a deafening roar as it exploded. The result was a ghastly sight, for it had landed right in the centre of the forward company of that Battalion and practically wiped it out. Had we gone ahead, as we might so easily have done, the catastrophe would have fallen on us, and my company would never have reported itself "present" at the rendezvous.

The scene around the outskirts and edge of Mametz Wood was simply indescribable. The whole place was literally carpeted with bodies, the enemy having put up an especially vigorous resistance in the attempt to hold the Wood. Considering that he was most thoroughly entrenched, and had the protection of the woods, it struck me as marvellous that our men had succeeded in winning.

They had had to rush over a wide stretch of absolutely open country without a particle of shelter except what was afforded by the shell holes, and it was uphill all the way from the road. What terrible execution they wrought among the enemy was very evident for the trenches were in many places piled three and four deep with bodies.

In the centre of this scene of carnage was our rendezvous. Owing to the fog two of the companies had lost their way, and we were delayed for an hour or more but eventually "all present" was reported and after eating a light lunch in this gruesome setting we moved forward once more. Our orders were to proceed to Bazentin-le-Petit and take up a position in front of the village at a given place. The Germans had very recently been driven out of the village and were attacking it in considerable force, so it looked as though we were in for some fun.

In less than an hour we reached the lower corner of Bazentin-le-Petit Wood and there rested for ten minutes. Our position gave us a splendid view of the village we were to hold. It also gave us a view which was by no means splendid of a very fine assortment of shells, large venomous ones, bursting incessantly all over the said village; evidently the Hun did not propose that we should occupy the place with any undue degree of comfort. "Marked activity" might be the description of the enemy's attitude. From every direction came the roar of shells and the spiteful crackling of machine guns. The whole air vibrated with the ceaseless noise. It was a beautiful Summer day completely spoilt. We made our way up the steep hill by way of the road that skirts the Eastern side of the wood and leads to the village, and I confess it looked as though we were walking straight into the jaws of death. Surely no one could come out of such an infernal bombardment.

By good luck we reached the village without a casualty and made our way along the shattered main street which ran through the ruined mass of buildings. On our left was the poor little church with only one small piece of wall standing, and on that, in a niche stood a statue of the Virgin with hands extended as though in welcome to us.

We halted just beyond the church while the Colonel and Adjutant went ahead to see about the position which had been assigned to us in the apple orchard. As a quartet of large shells burst rather too close, sending bricks and earth hurtling through the air, the order was given to take what cover was available. The best protection to be found was in shell holes. There was an abundant supply of these, and more were being made every minute. Here and there a ruined house or cellar would offer some inducement, but though this afforded protection against pieces of flying metal or bricks, it also afforded a most excellent opportunity for inexpensive and very expeditious burial.

It was not long before the Colonel returned with information of a most unsatisfactory nature. The position allotted to us was so crowded with men that not another one could be crowded in. This meant that for the present at least we must remain where we were. As a health resort the place could by no stretch of the imagination be considered a success, and we all sincerely hoped our term of occupation would be short.

The Colonel, second in command, and Adjutant were in a nice shell hole on the side of the main street, I with about fifteen men occupied the adjoining one. In front of us was a bank of earth some ten feet high. About us the rest of the battalion were crouching in all sorts of places, but the shell holes were I think the most popular. Frequent moves became necessary as the enemy picked out certain spots for his kindly attentions and the moves were made with extraordinary speed.

The number of shells that entered the ruined village was appalling, and the incessant roar absolutely deafening. Every now and then the explosions would send masses of earth and débris among us, while great pieces of metal shrieked past in a most disconcerting way. Under such conditions it seemed impossible that we could escape destruction and I do not believe any one of us expected to see another day. Names and addresses of wives or mothers were written on scraps of paper and passed from one to another with the simple request: "If I get scuppered send a line to this address, you know what to say." "Right oh! you might do the same for me like a good chap." That was all, no one seemed astonished or excited at the predicament we were in. It was part of the game and perhaps the worst part because at the present time we were not able to hit back.

Occasionally a groan showed that some fellow bad been hit, and the others in the shell hole would crouch a little lower. Our Major who was sitting next to me was hit twice on his "tin hat" but neither time did the metal go through the tough steel. Had he not been wearing that hat he would most certainly have been killed. Then a third piece struck the hat, a tiny splinter of hard metal, it penetrated and cut a long furrow the entire length of his head, fortunately not breaking the skull. A few minutes later a large shell burst on the opposite side of the street and the Adjutant leaned back, stone dead. I could scarcely believe that poor S—— was gone. He was such a good chap! Of our old lot that had trained together in England except myself, and I was fast becoming useless owing to the effect of the gas which was getting in its deadly work and causing me very great pain, there was now only one unwounded officer left.

The long strain and the many casualties, to say nothing of the frequent partial buryings, were beginning to tell on the men, and the Colonel thought it advisable to calm them. Before we realised what he was doing he was out of the shell hole and on the bullet-swept street. With the utmost calmness he took out a cigarette from his case, lit it, and walked up and down the *pavé* smoking away as though he were on Pall Mall. Why he was not killed the good Lord only knows. By all the laws of chance he should have been riddled, but no, the cigarette finished, he rejoined us in the hole and had the satisfaction of observing that the men had quieted down. It was a splendidly brave thing to do. Later he acknowledged that he had been "in a deuce of a funk."

This incident shows something of the relationship between the men and the officers in our army. It is the officers' duty to understand the psychology of the men, to know when to give orders and when to get things done by setting an example. When to be harsh, when to be lenient. In other words he must *know* men and in particular those under his own command, know them individually, their personal peculiarities, their weak points and their strong points, and he must make the men respect him while he in turn respects them. Here lies the chief difference between our army and the Germans. They *drive* their men, we *lead* ours not only into battle but in other things. People laugh at us for our peculiar habit of going over the top carrying walking sticks. This has a moral effect that cannot be overestimated. To those who question it, there is this answer: the men follow.

It is very different from the German method. The officer goes behind his men. He is in the safer position, and the very idea of an officer being safer than his men is abhorrent to us and contrary to all our traditions. The question of the officers' personal relations with the men is always interesting but very difficult to define. The line between fellowship and familiarity is most sharply drawn, even under the strain of life at the fighting front it seldom breaks down; this is due chiefly to our mutual respect. We know that the men will do anything they are told to do and endure the utmost hardships without complaint. They in turn know that the officer will never ask them to take unnecessary risks and will always consider their welfare before his own.

After a long march when all are equally tired (the officers carry full equipment except rifle and cartridges, but have other things in their place) when the officer is, perhaps even more tired as he has the strain of the responsibility in addition to the physical fatigue. He must not think of attending to his own comforts until he has seen that the men are properly cared for. This often requires many hours of work and much walking when he would much rather be resting.

As time went on things instead of getting better grew steadily worse. If we remained much longer there would be no battalion to take away. So after a brief consultation the Colonel decided to go out ahead with the Major, who was feeling very groggy, while I was to take the men out of the village to a place of comparative safety near the Wood. It was necessary to proceed slowly, as any quick movement would have looked like a panic, and so, perhaps, have started trouble. But to march out slowly under such heavy shell fire was not quite as easy as it sounds. Three of the companies got out more or less intact. Then a large tree was struck by a shell and fell across the roadway and held up the last company which was in charge of young W——. The brief delay was fatal, for a big shell landed in the midst of the company and caused a terrible number of casualties, among them poor W——. He and I had been platoon commanders together in England and I felt his death very keenly, his extraordinary coolness and courage had earned the highest admiration from all who knew him.

The Brigadier on hearing the C.O.'s account told us to take up a position near the main road in Death's Valley and hold ourselves in readiness to move forward at a moment's notice to the ridge alongside of the village we had just left, as there was a good deal happening up there, and reinforcements might be needed very soon. The valley in which we were to wait was being shelled pretty freely, so the men were ordered to dig in.

Now if there is one order which never has to be repeated it is "Dig in." In an incredibly short time the red clay ground was honey-combed with holes big enough to hold one or two men. Those holes are most comfortable things and give one a feeling of safety if not of luxury. Of course they cannot be depended on to protect you if a shell, whether it be large or small, insists on sharing the hole, it is then quite time to look for "a better 'ole." The Colonel insisted on appointing me Adjutant, a post I have never wanted to fill, but there was no help for it and I had to accept. In fact I was feeling too ill to care much what I was or did. The gas was getting in its deadly work. My career during the past ten days had been one of many changes. Brigade Scout and Intelligence Officer, Second in Command. Company Commander and Adjutant, and all this time my official rank (*and* pay) was that of Lieutenant.

In the course of the afternoon we were ordered to send a company into Bazentin-le-Petit in order to capture or destroy some enemy machine guns that had been playing havoc. It was a nasty undertaking, but young A——, a mere boy of 19 years, made a satisfactory job of it and returned without having had any casualties. While we lay in our various earthly grave-like receptacles watching the continued bombarding of Bazentin-le-Petit and thanking our stars that we were not in that death trap, we were interested in seeing the - cavalry passing along the road. They had been at Delville Wood, or as Tommy calls it "Devil Wood." As they rode along, the Germans, evidently knowing the route they would take and their approximate pace, followed them with shells all the way down, almost as far as Fricourt, but as good luck would have it they always overshot the mark by seventy-five or a hundred yards. Just like the Germans, if they do a thing wrong they keep on doing it wrong, thinking that because *they* do it, it must be right. Their first range had been wrong by a certain amount, and the error had continued as long as they followed the road. We were not sorry to see the last of these horsemen as they had been the innocent cause of a number of shells dropping in our particular neighbourhood.

Late that evening things quieted down. The Hun had had enough, and was content to leave us in possession of all we had acquired, and as our Battalion were not likely to be needed we received the welcome orders to return to Bottom Wood, and so, wearily, and sadly depleted in numbers, we retraced our steps to our starting point of the morning. During our absence the woods and small valley beyond had been heavily *strafed*, but comparative quiet now reigned, and we were glad to be back, not even objecting to the filthy tear gas which filled the air. For my own part I could not have kept going any longer. The gas was affecting my lungs and heart and an incessant cough racked me so that I could scarcely lie down. The stuffy gas-laden air of the dugout made things worse, and never do I remember having spent a more miserable night. As Adjutant it was important that I attended to certain duties the following morning, but I fear that my reports were somewhat incoherent.

About noon orders came for us to move forward that night to take part in an attack. The doctor having forbidden my going, there was nothing for it but to make my way back to the hospital, which I proceeded to do as soon as I had attended to the Battalion's rations, and handed over the Adjutancy to one of the new officers.

That trip back to M——e was a nightmare. At first I tried to ride, but the horse loaned to me was a big powerful high-spirited animal; every time a gun fired, and it seemed as though the whole country was nothing but guns, the beast reared and made himself generally objectionable. After half an hour of this agony, as I was almost blinded with pain, I handed the horse over to one of the ration party and made the rest of the way on foot. The distance was only about three or four miles but it took me hours to do it. In vain did I examine each ambulance that passed, but they were crowded to the limit of their capacity with men in far worse condition than I was, for the past two days had been costly.

Occasionally along the road I came across others like myself, who were not considered bad enough for ambulances, and they hobbled along in every condition of body, some slightly and some quite badly wounded, some could only go a few steps between halts, others moved along almost gaily with broken arms or flesh wounds which did not prevent their walking. The great thing is to get to a hospital as soon as possible, have the wounds dressed and then on to "Blighty."

It was very late when I finally reached the hospital and there learned after examination that I had been gassed, and that I should not have taken a step since receiving the poison the day before.

Having been duly labelled and laid on a stretcher, I was put in a large ambulance and taken to H——y where there was a very large clearing hospital composed of innumerable tents. Never so long as I live shall I forget the feeling of contentment that followed the washing and careful kindly treatment given to me by those splendid nurses, and the nice comfortable bed, with its sweet clean sheets. It was Heaven, and the nurses were the angels. It was worth all the horrors of the past days, and what those horrors were I have scarcely suggested as they would not make good reading. Even though sleep was impossible, I enjoyed lying there, quite satisfied that I did not have to move, that no one expected me to do anything, that there was no insistent telephone giving unwelcome orders, and best of all that there were no shells and no gas. In my semi-stupefied condition it mattered not to me that in the cots around me men were dying. At least their last minutes were made as painless and comfortable as possible, poor fellows, for them the war was over, they had given their all, and they could face their Maker with the knowledge that they had done their full duty. The following evening I was taken to the train. Things are rather vague in my mind regarding the next few hours, dimly I recall the wonderful hospital train where everything that can be done for the comfort of the wounded is so faithfully done by those who serve under the Red Cross.

My destination was Rouen, one of those splendid hospitals where the same kindness and efficiency are so noticeable. Owing to the urgency of keeping hospitals in France as clear as possible for bad cases that cannot bear travelling, all who can be moved are sent to England, and I was very happy when one morning a few days later the nurse came in, accompanied by stretcher bearers, and informed me that I was to go to "Blighty."

How or by what route I was going did not interest me, it was sufficient that I would soon be HOME. To my surprise the ambulance took me down to the river; and alongside of the landing was a beautiful white steamer with a broad green band and a very large Red Cross painted on the side, the markings of a hospital ship, supposed to protect it against attack, but the German disregards that law as he does so many others. On to this steamer I was carried, and within an hour we started down that wonderful quiet river. What a day that was, glorious mid-summer weather and England only a few hours away! Life was worth while after all.

Chapter XVI
The Pivot

IT TURNED OUT that my days at the front were finished, that I was considered unfit for further active service so far as the trenches were concerned. In some ways I regret that fact, for with all the horrors, all the hardships, there is a fascination about the life over there that cannot be described. Not for all the money on earth would I have missed the experience of those days. Many things were taught, but none more thoroughly than the admiration for Tommy Atkins. He is a *man* through and through. He grumbles and he growls, especially when things are going too well, but he does his job.

It is hard luck not being in the active part of the "show" until the end, but unfortunately that has been the fate of so many and we who are alive and free from serious mutilation are among the lucky ones, notwithstanding the fact that we are out of the fight itself. We can look back at the Battle of the Somme with a great satisfaction, for even though we were unable to go forward as far as it was hoped we might, we demonstrated beyond any doubt the efficiency of our new army. We showed the Germans that even with the training of a year or so our men were a match for their highly trained, machine-made soldiers.

Germany, when she selected the Somme region for her great strategic line of resistance (after being forced back from her drive to Paris) had done all that human ingenuity could do to render her line impregnable. It was called a trench system but more correctly speaking it was a system of underground and ground-level forts, with reinforced concrete construction at the vital points, subterranean passages and immense assembly dugouts, barbed wire entanglements on a scale never before attempted, guns and machine guns in numbers hitherto unknown. Nothing had been left to chance.

But in spite of all these gigantic preparations and precautions, our long months of seeming inertia, during which we were quietly making ready, Germany's armies were forced to retire before the advance of our men, forced to relinquish line after line, to acknowledge at last that we were not only their equals but their superiors in the game of fighting. Germany had prayed for *Der Tag* and she got it on July 1st, 1916, though not in the way she expected it, for on that memorable day we started to win - to break the power of the greatest military organisation that the world has ever known. It was the pivotal day of the war. As we look back and see how from the beginning of the Battle of the Somme our armies have forged ahead in France, at the thousands of square miles of territory the invaders have been forced to abandon, at the hundreds of villages returned to France, some mere masses of ruin, others more or less intact, at the thousands of prisoners we have captured, and find that with one slight exception all our gains have been held, we feel that our efforts have not been in vain, and that eventually the great military power of Germany will be broken.

The recent developments in Russia appear to be very discouraging, but against the bad news from that quarter we have the magnificent co-operation of the United States. Her unlimited resources in men, money and material - the three great M's - will prove to be a factor of the most vital importance - that she will throw the entire weight of her gigantic power into the task of freeing the world from any risk of the tryranny of German domination is certain and Germany will most bitterly regret the acts, such as the sinking of the *Lusitania*, which brought America into the war.

In the months that have passed since the days of the Somme, I have listened to too much talk. I have read even more of what men think. Many are too willing and free with their criticism. These critics are divided into two classes: destructive and constructive. The former by far the larger, and they again are divided into two parties: those who have entered the service of their country in a moment of transient patriotism, filled with desire to be seen in King's uniform, these may have been kept in England owing to their inefficiency in some way or other, or they may have gone to France, or one of the other fronts, and failed to make good. They growl without ceasing, and find fault with everything and everybody, especially those who, by their greater ability, have attained higher rank. Nothing is being done right and no one who has succeeded in gaining distinction is any good at all, so they say. Then the other lot are those who sit smugly in their arm chairs and tell how the war should be conducted, and how and why this or that offensive failed. They know it all, and their foolish prattle tests the patience of ail who hear it. For them death is almost too good. They are a scourge, and the world is not big enough to hold them. Their insolence in criticising the magnificent work that is being done makes one's blood boil. Let them give up their comforts for a bit and go over to France and see what *men* do. Let them see the difficulties that continually confront those who are in power out there. Let them taste of the Hunnish Horrors, then perhaps they will put a seal on their tongues and unlock their minds.

This is no time for finding fault, for trying to undermine the trust of the people in those who are making the Herculean efforts that have surprised the world. It is time for doing things, great or small according to the individual ability. If every one will do his utmost and keep his tongue in check, our task will be the easier. We shall shorten the days of the war, and will reap the benefits for which we have shed our blood and treasure.